CHINA NAKED

Frank Rothe

CHINA NAKED

Contributions by / Beiträge von

Celina Lunsford

Frank Rothe

Christoph Tannert

KEHRER

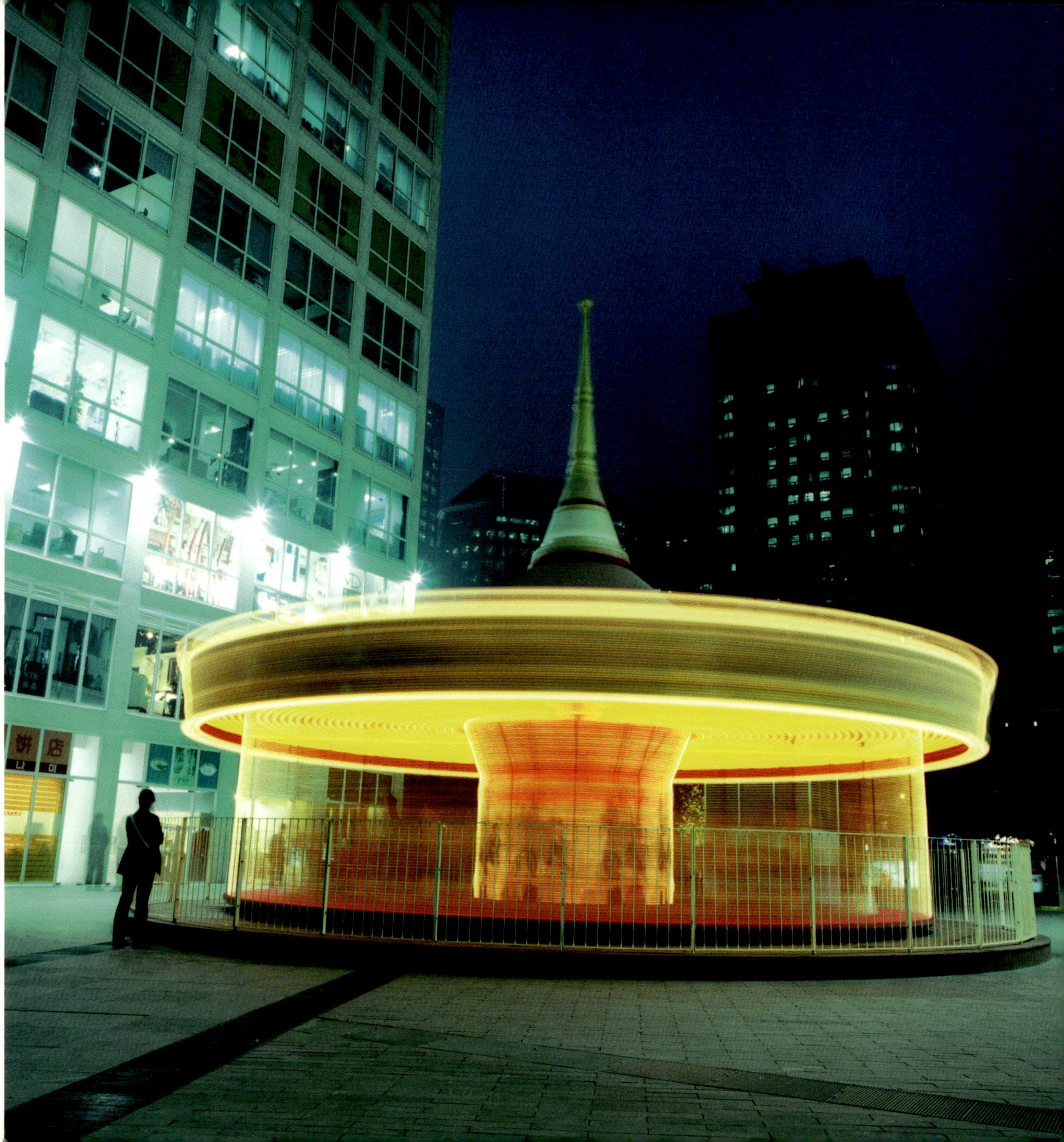

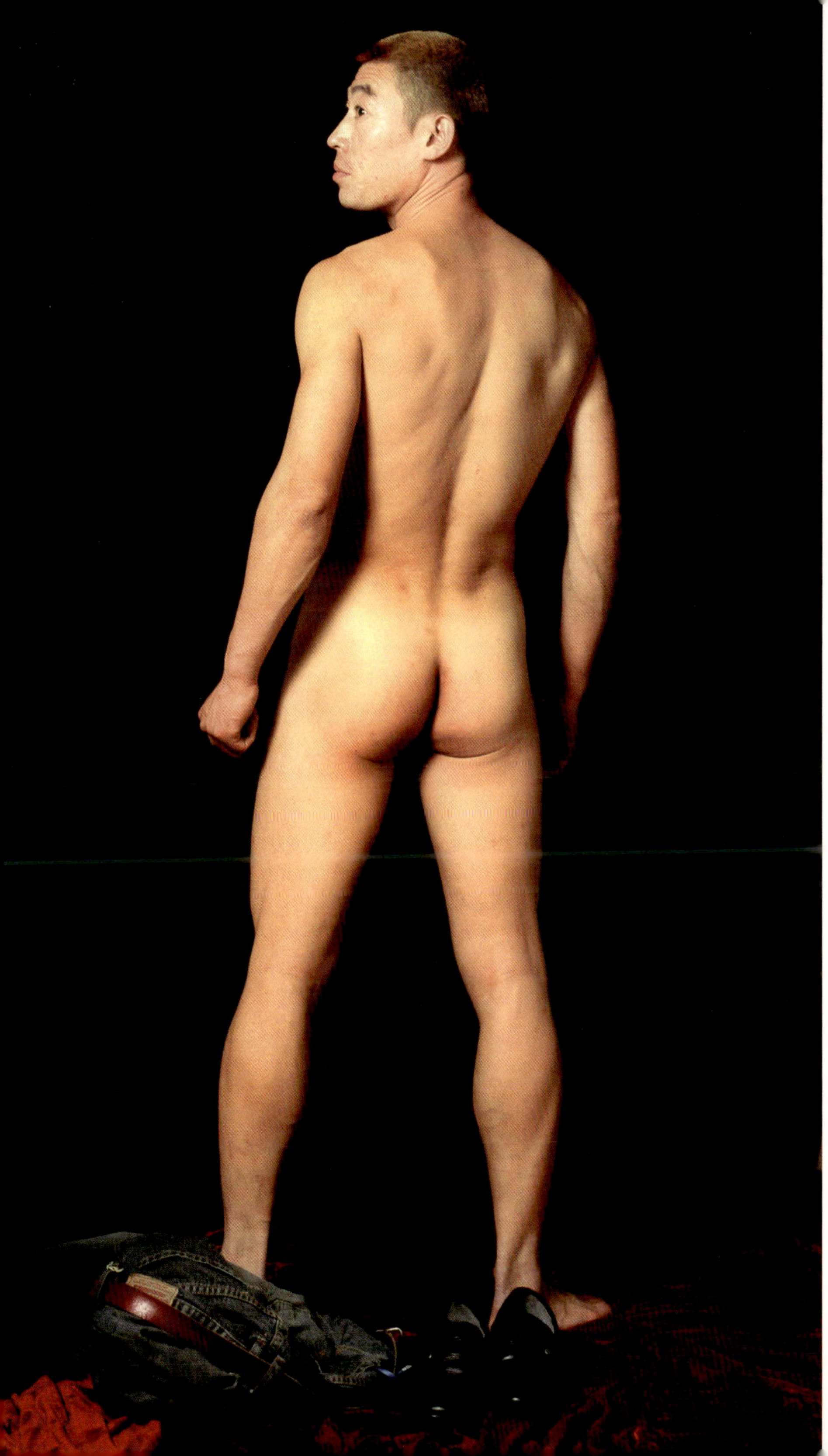

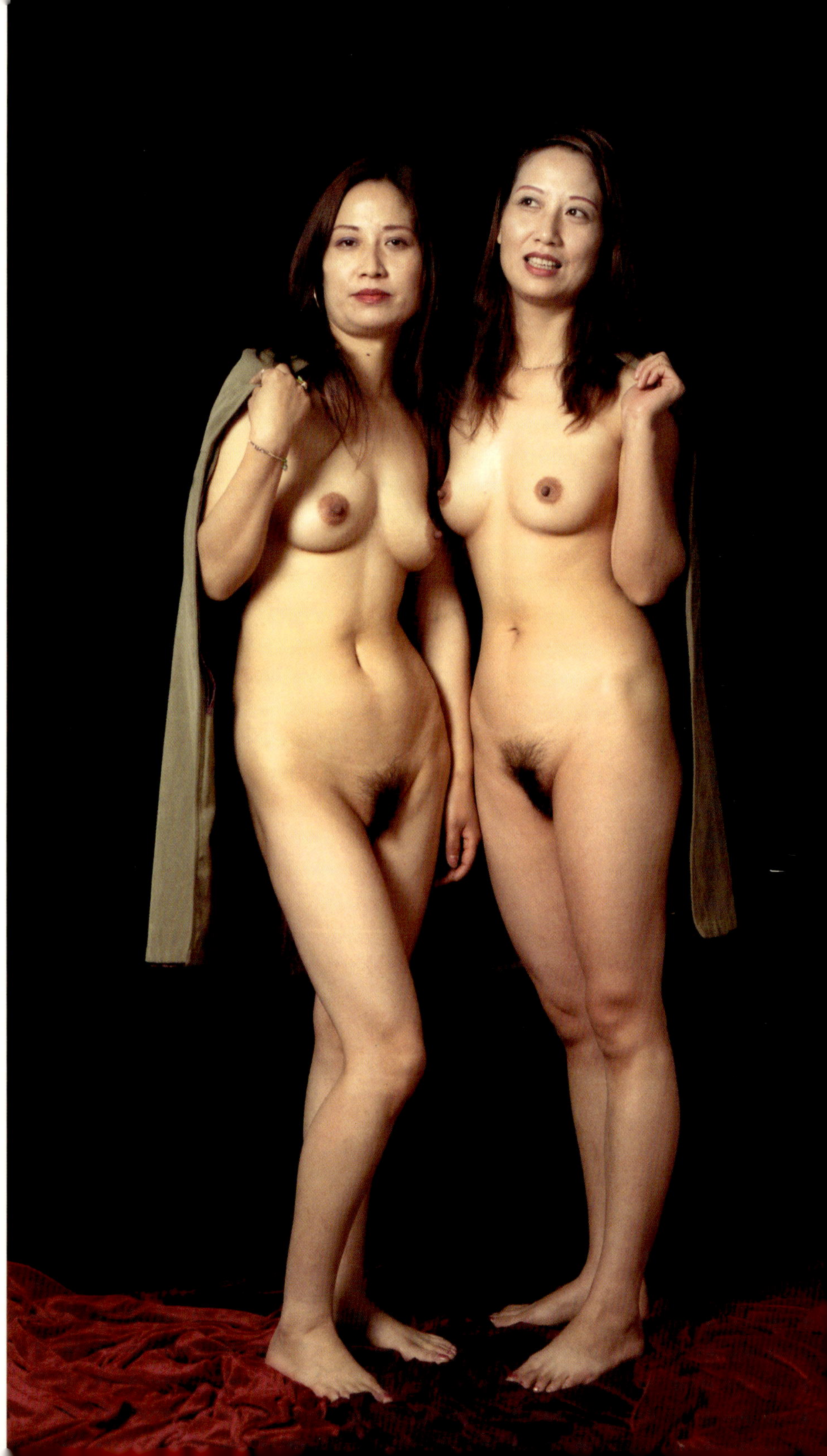

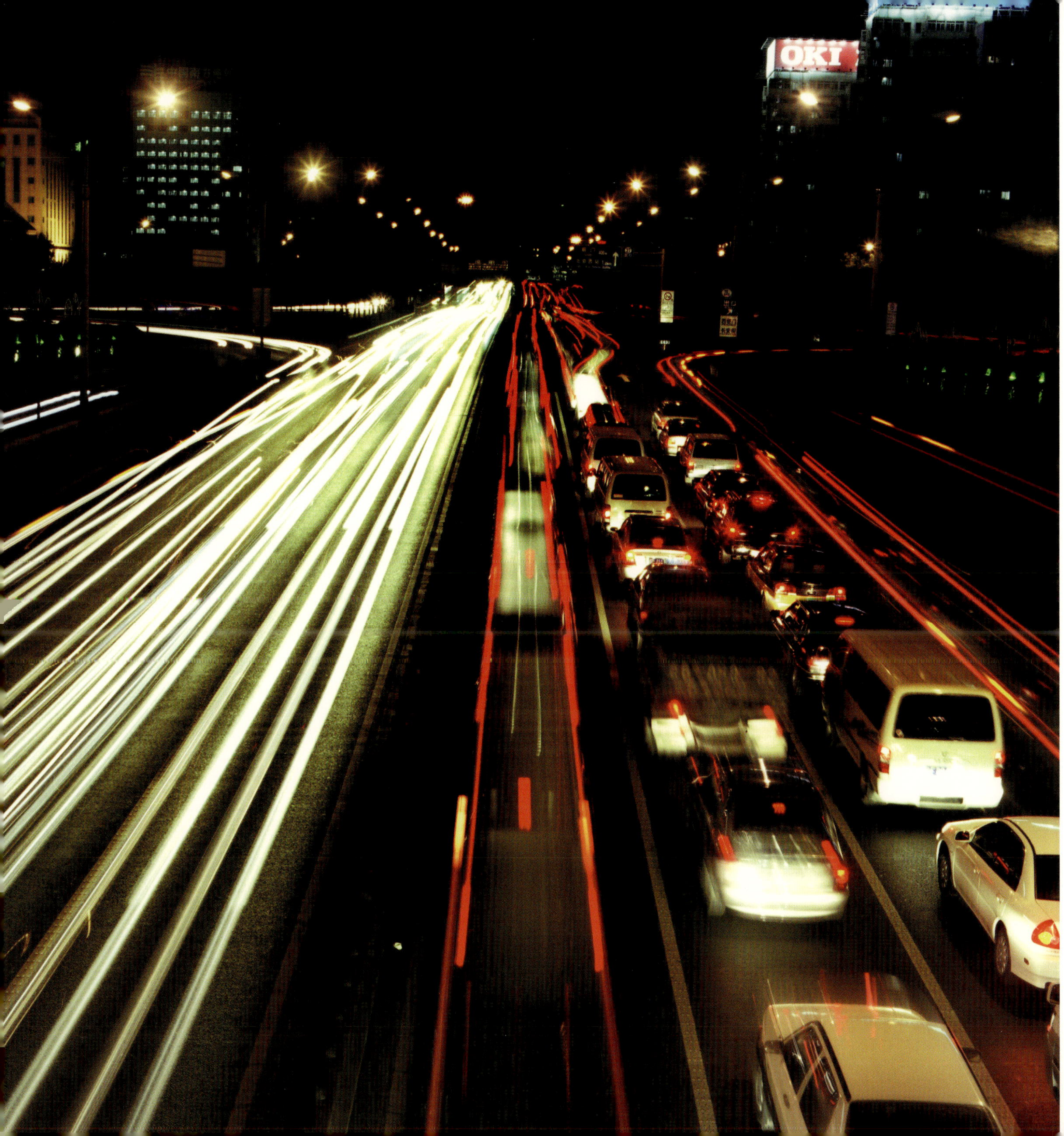
OKI

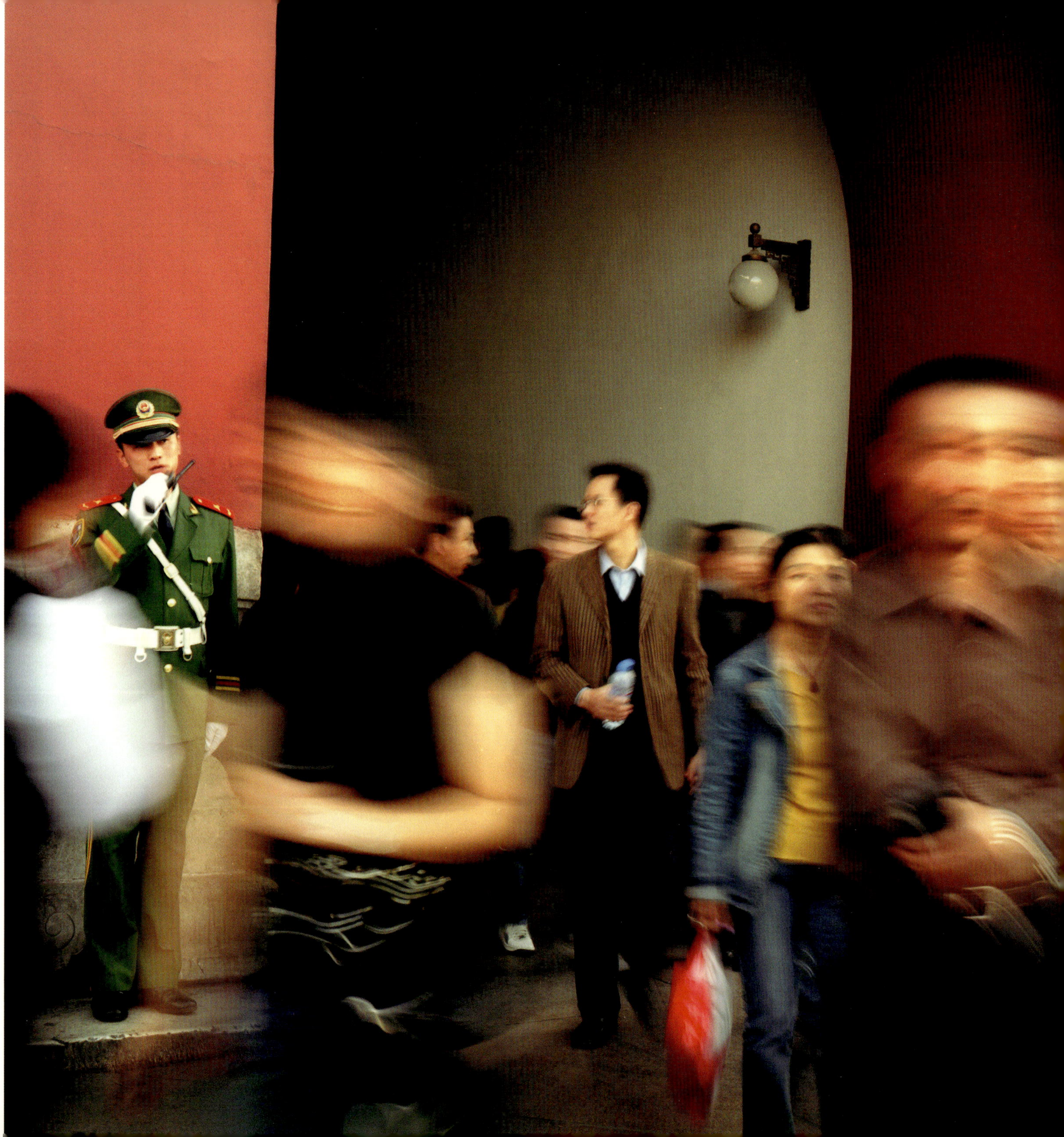

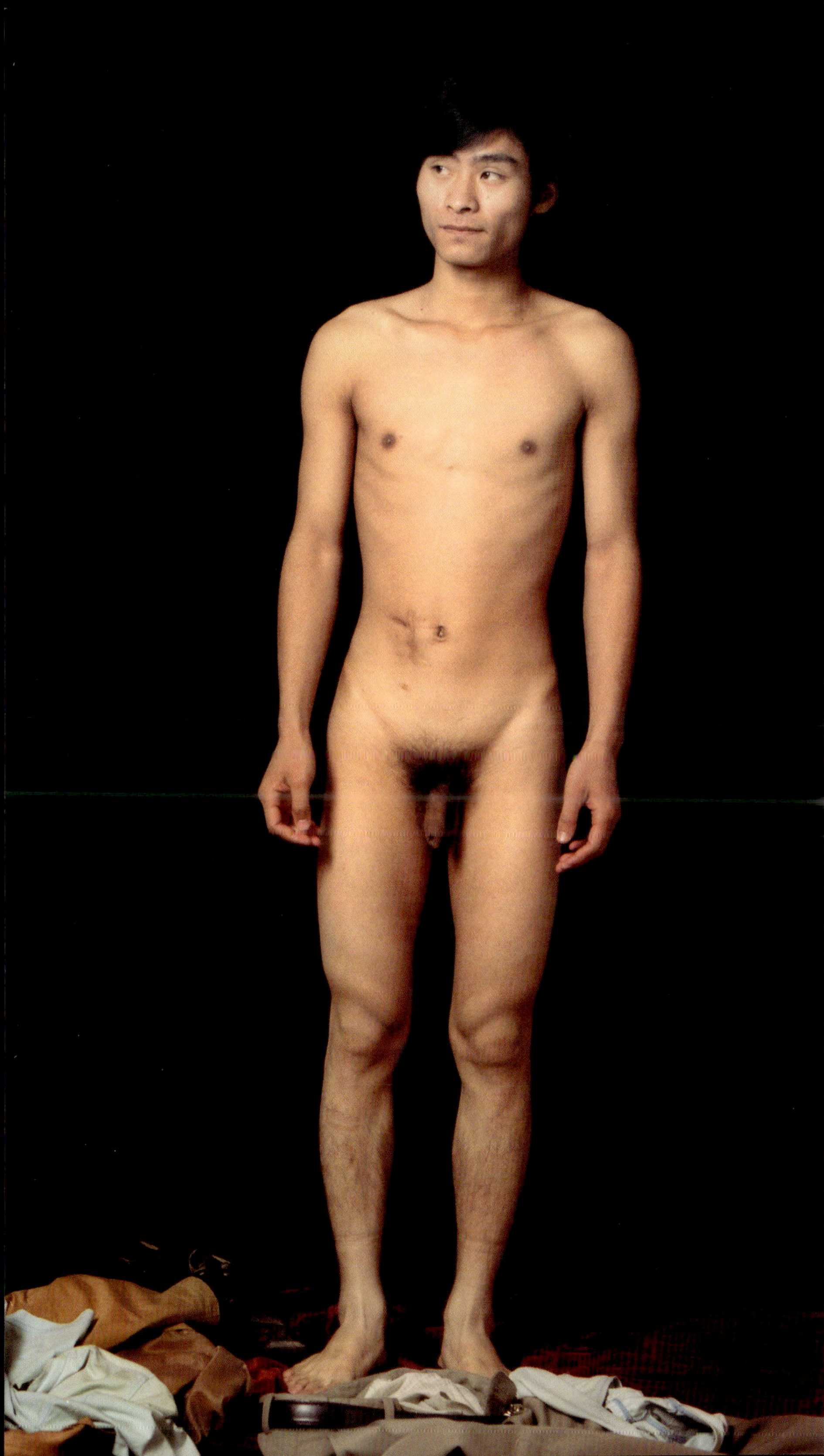

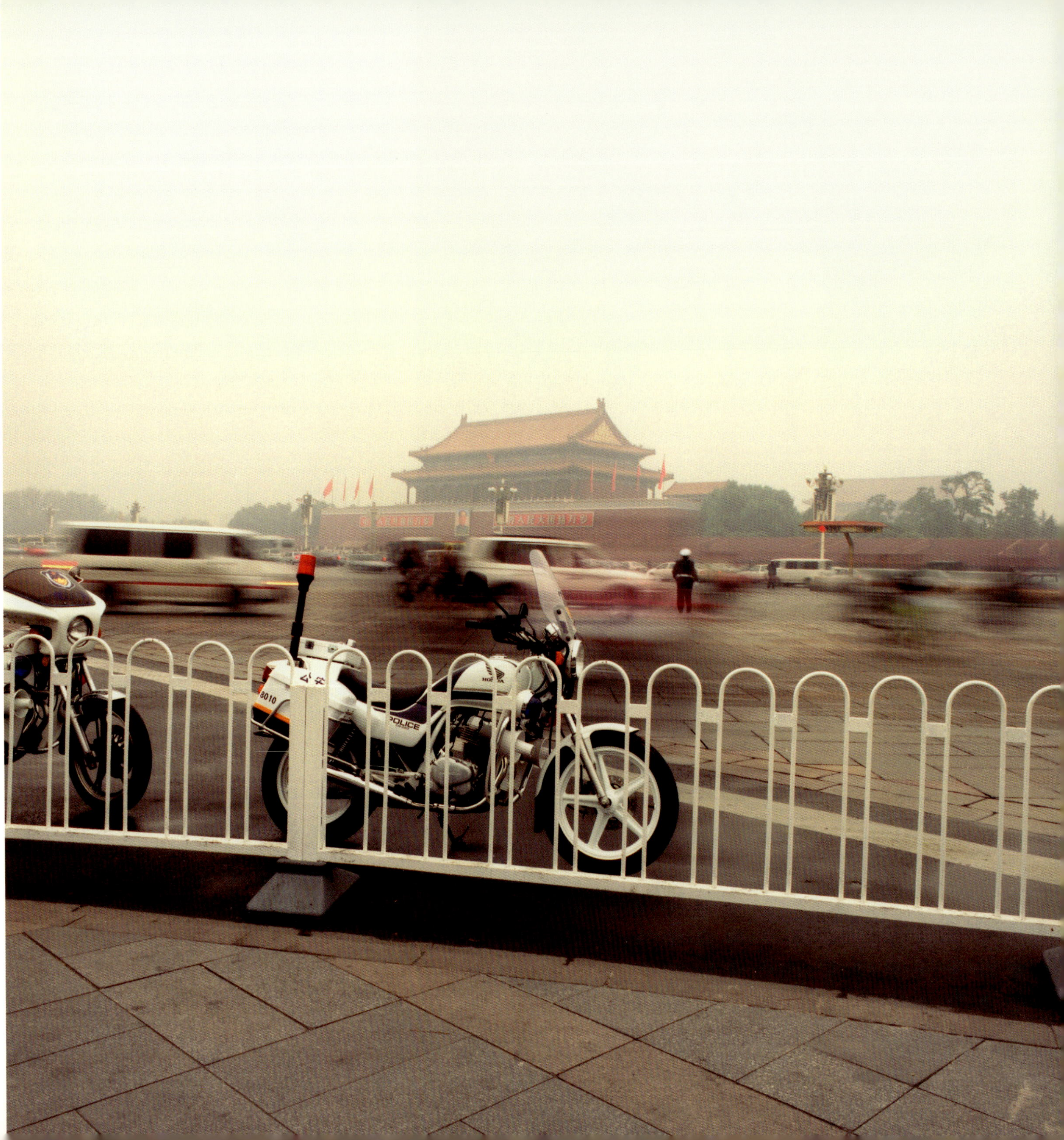
8010
POLICE

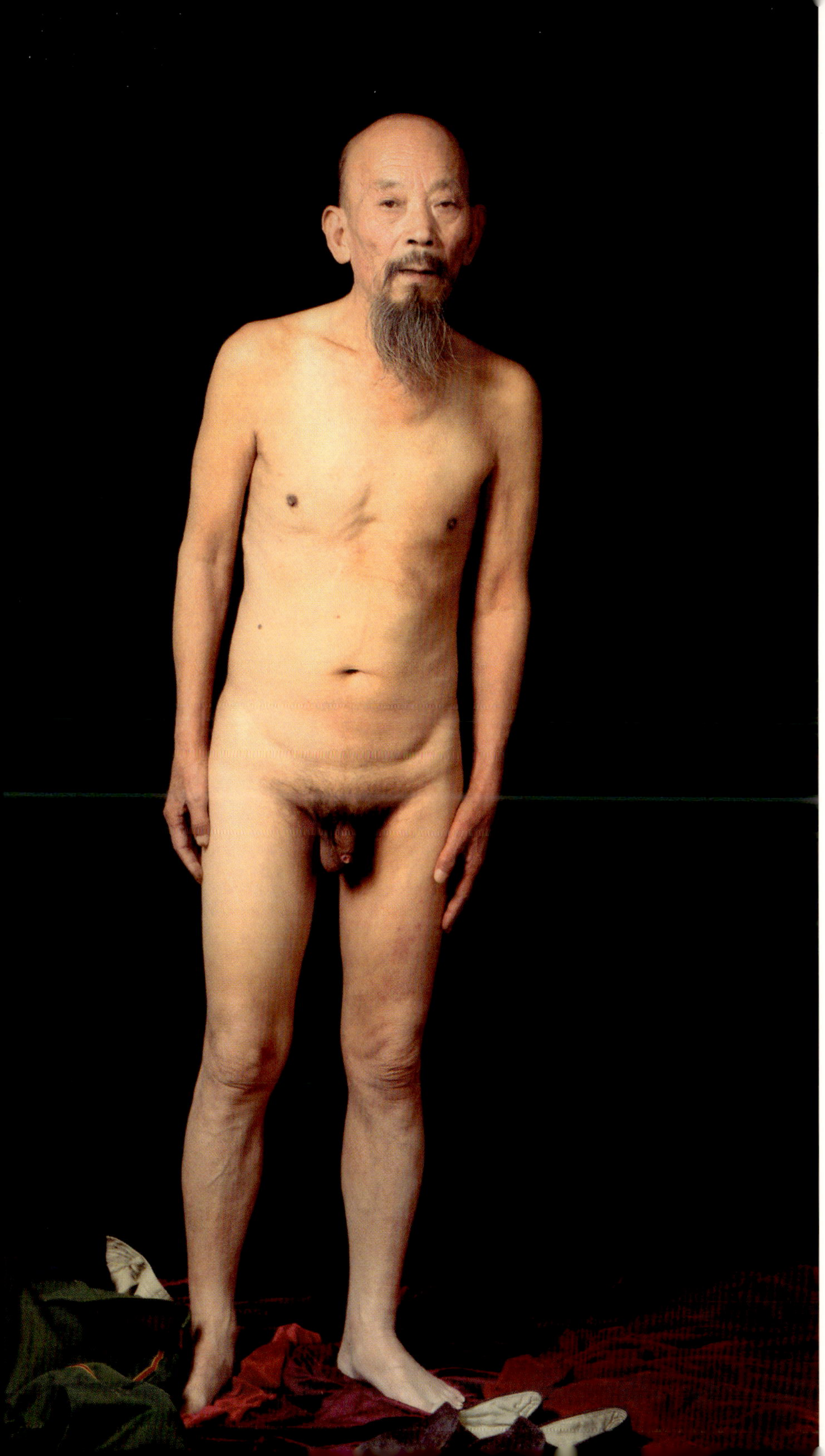

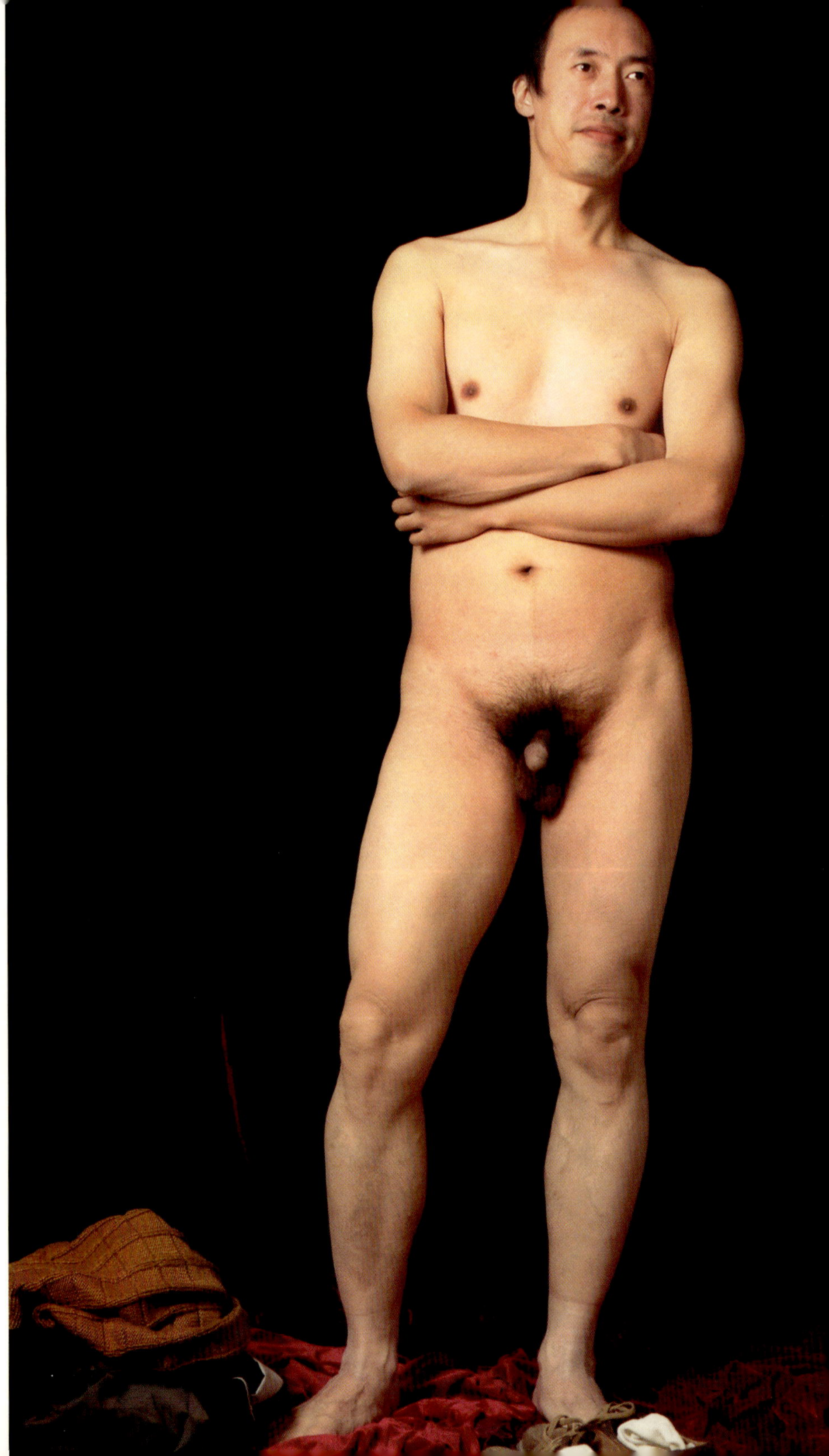

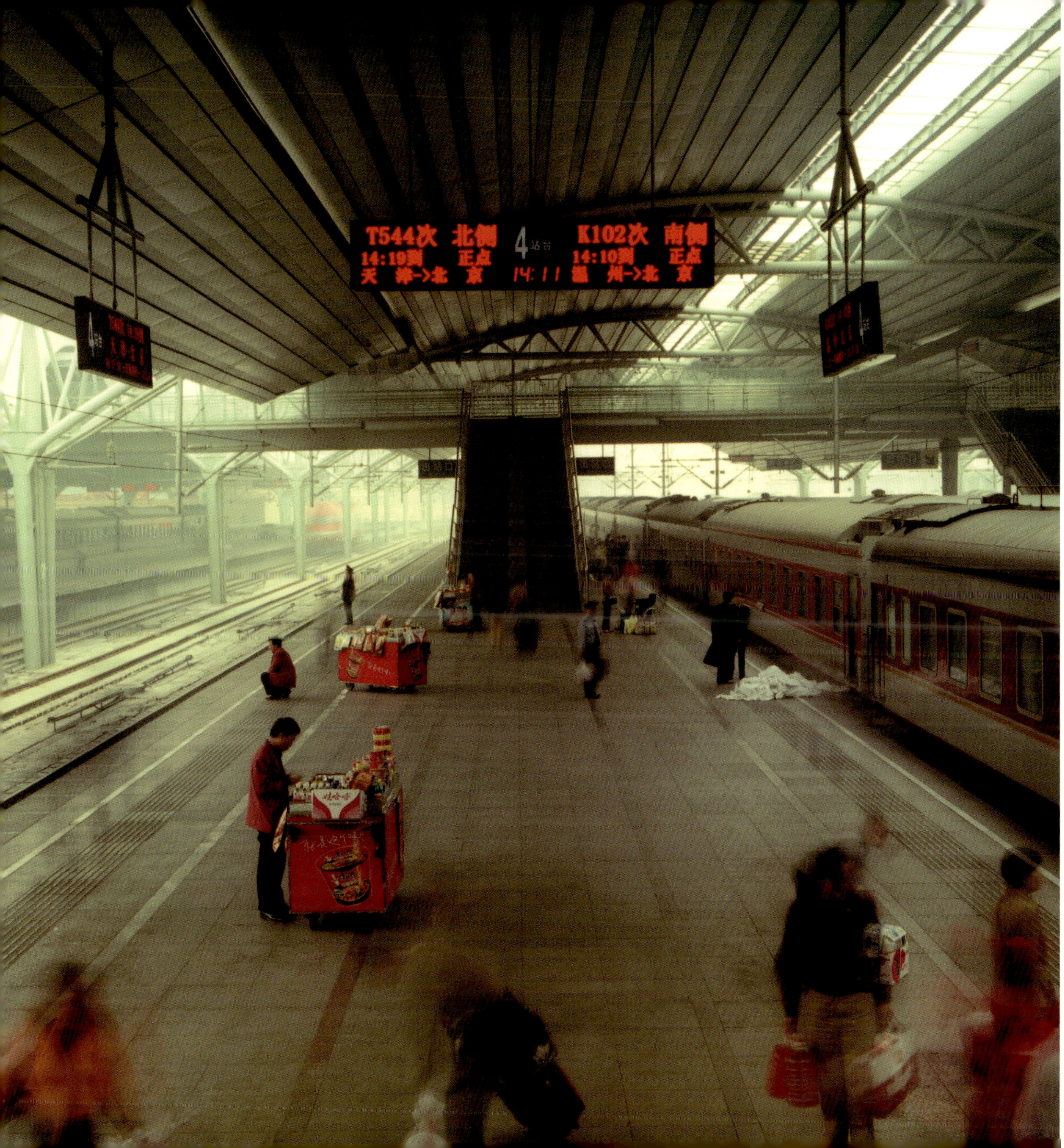
T544次 北侧 4站台 K102次 南侧
14:19到 正点 14:10到 正点
天 津->北 京 14:11 福 州->北 京

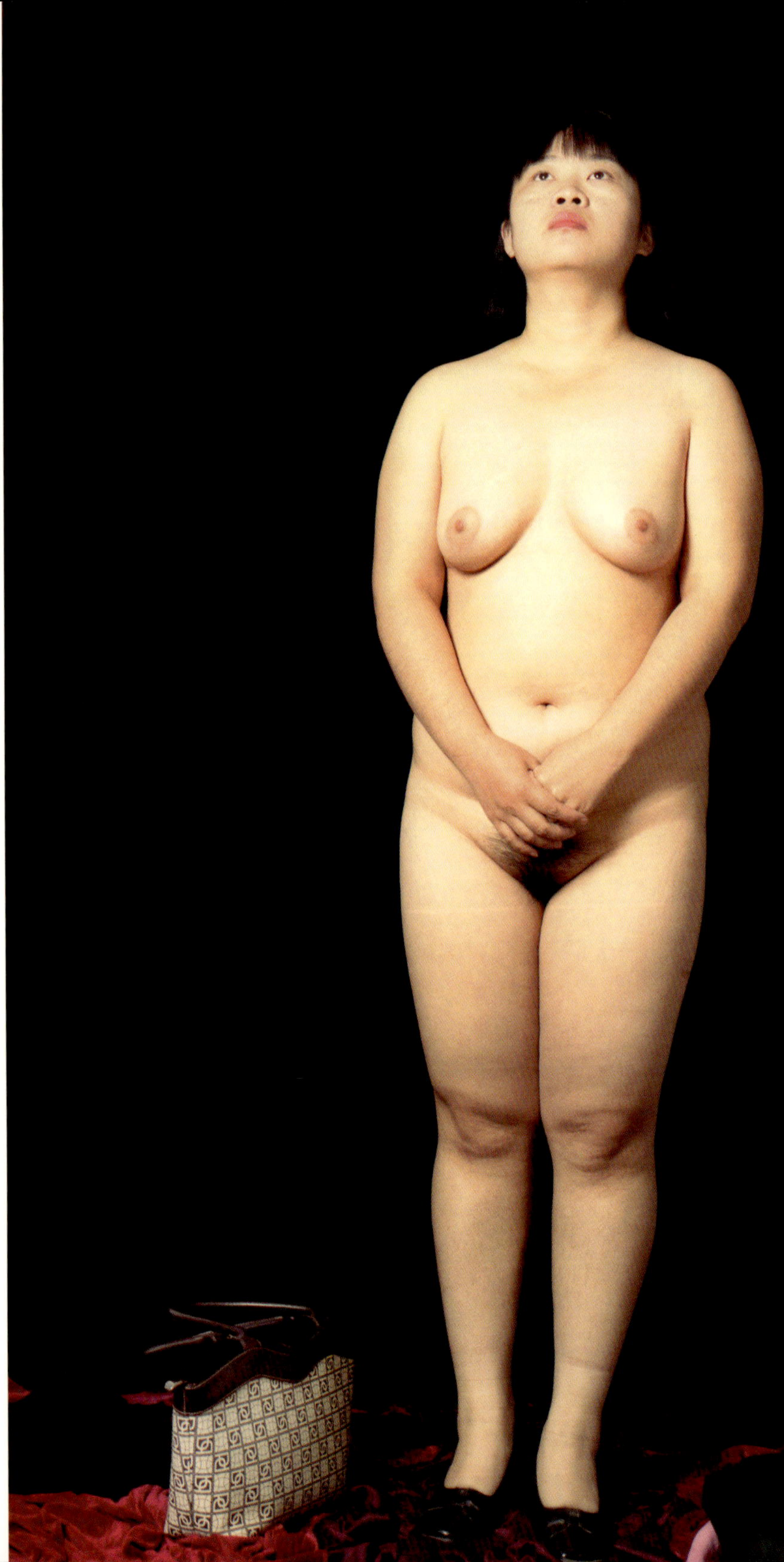

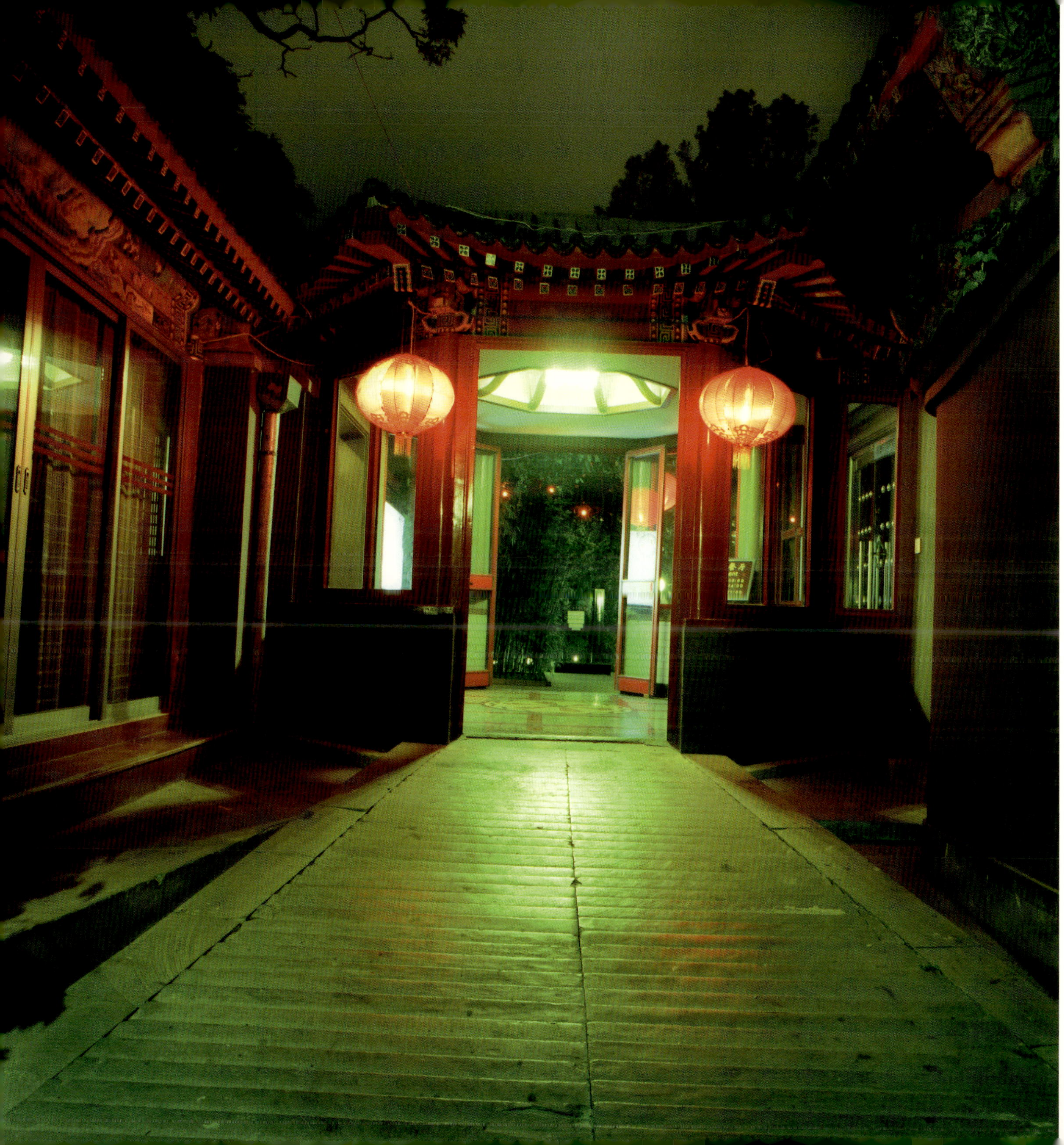

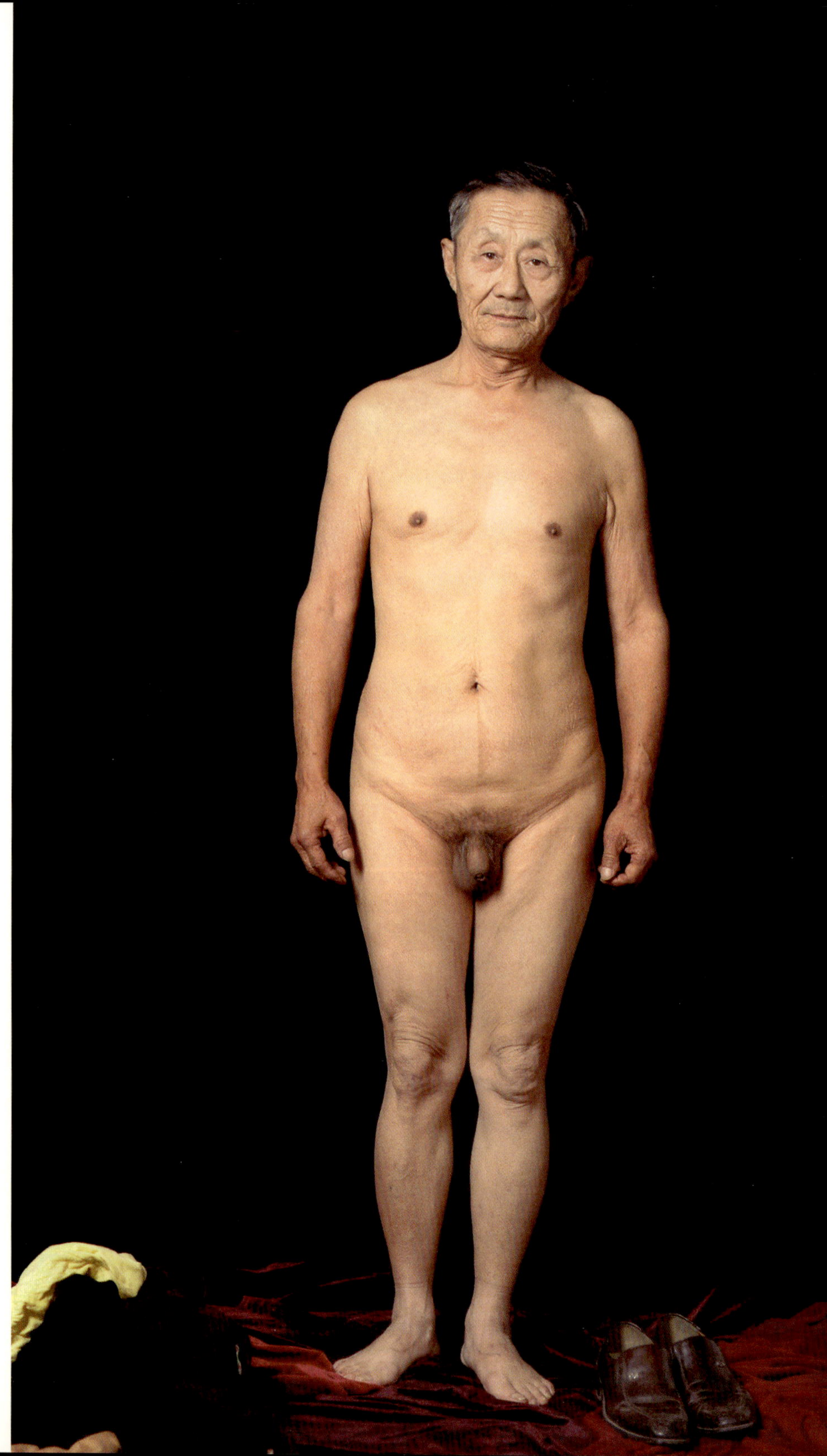

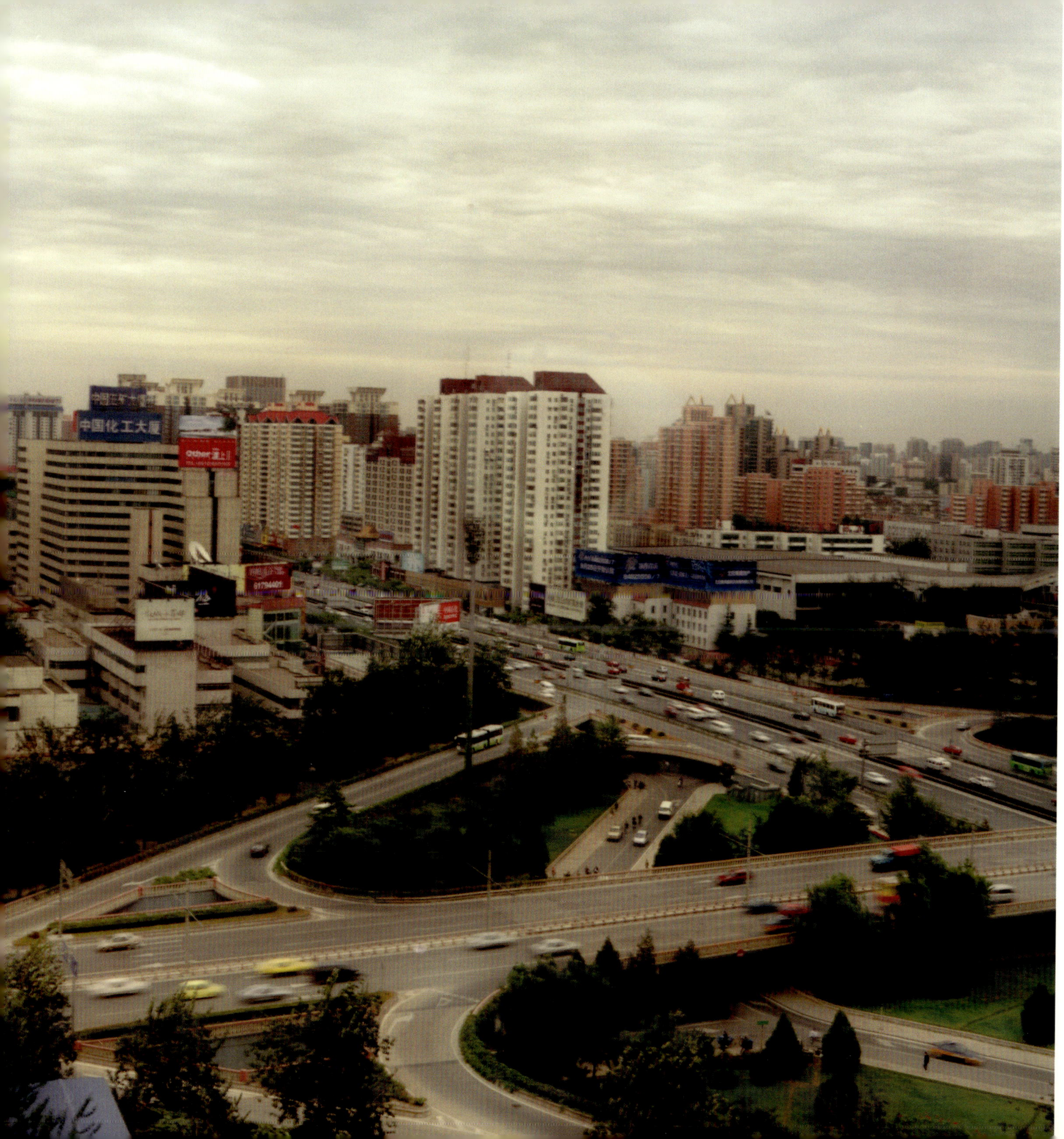
中国化工大厦

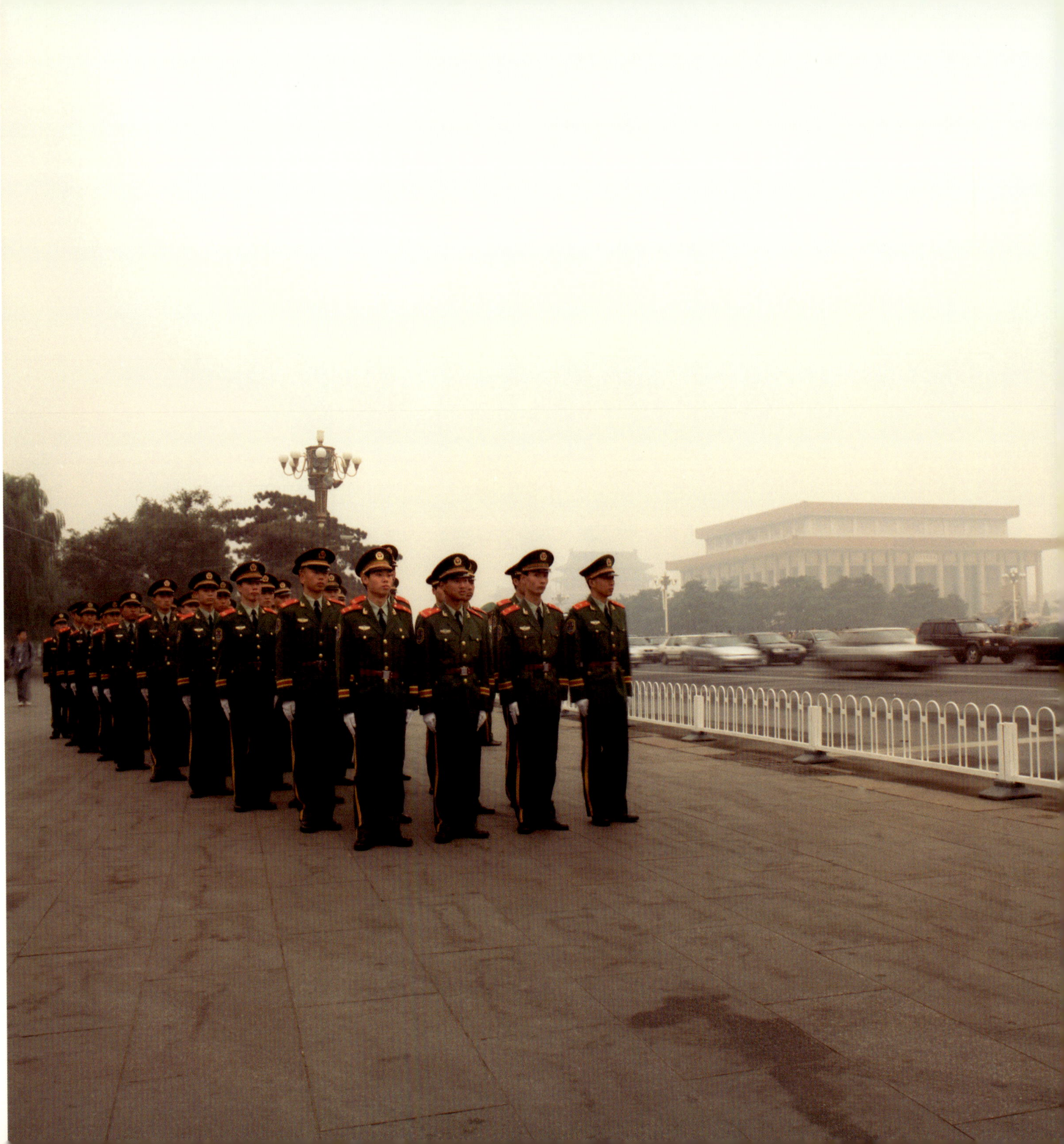

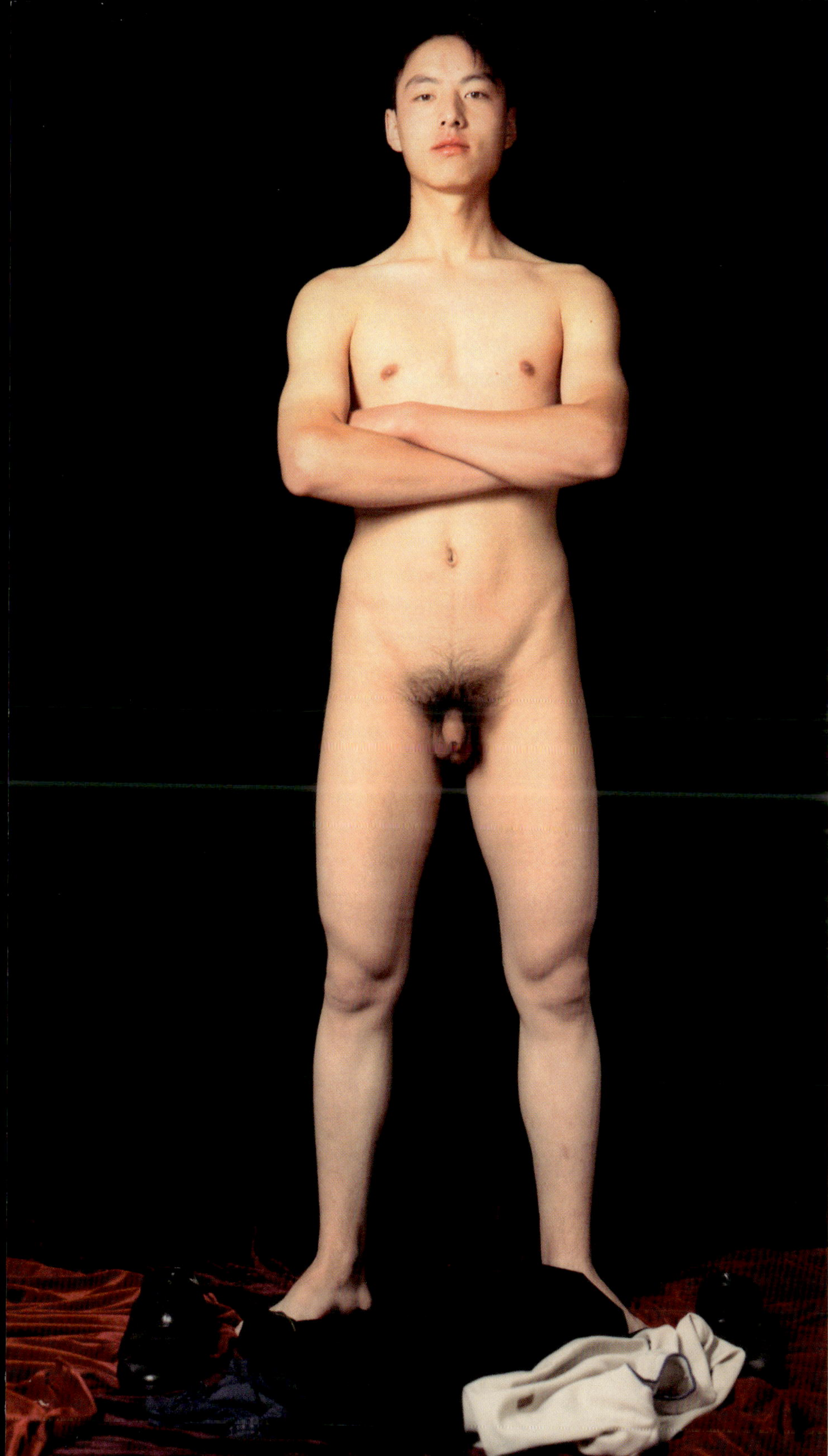

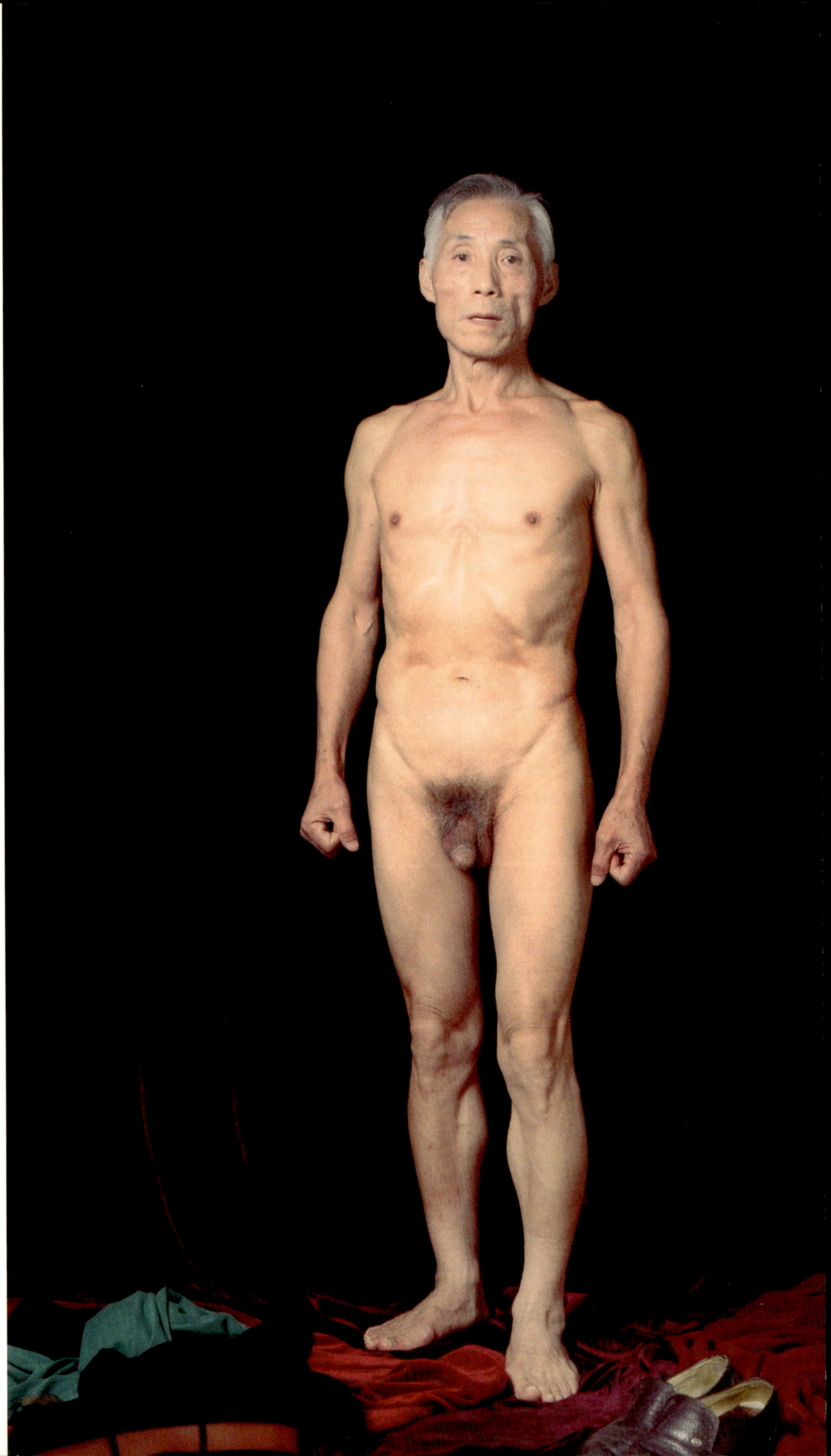

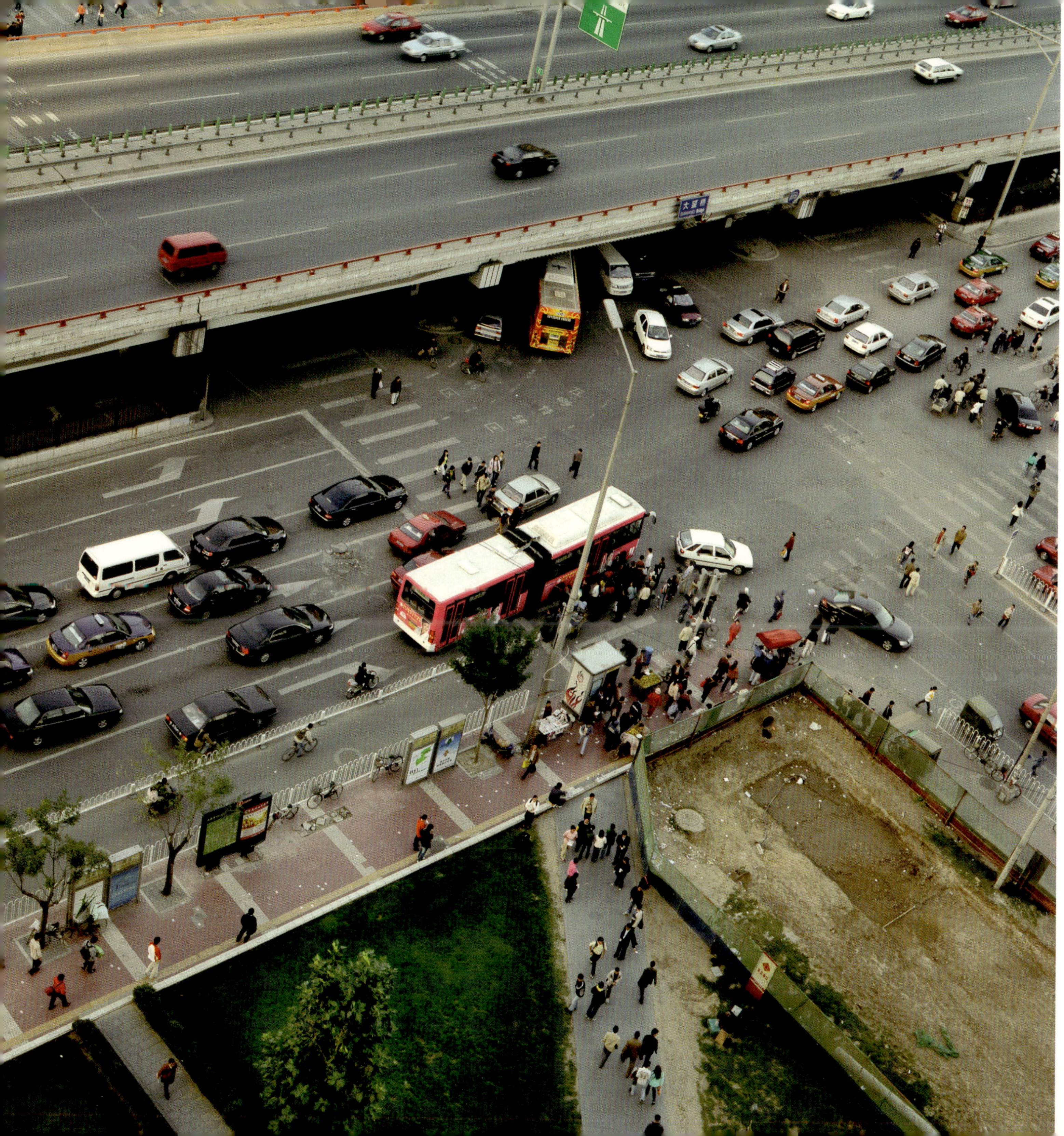

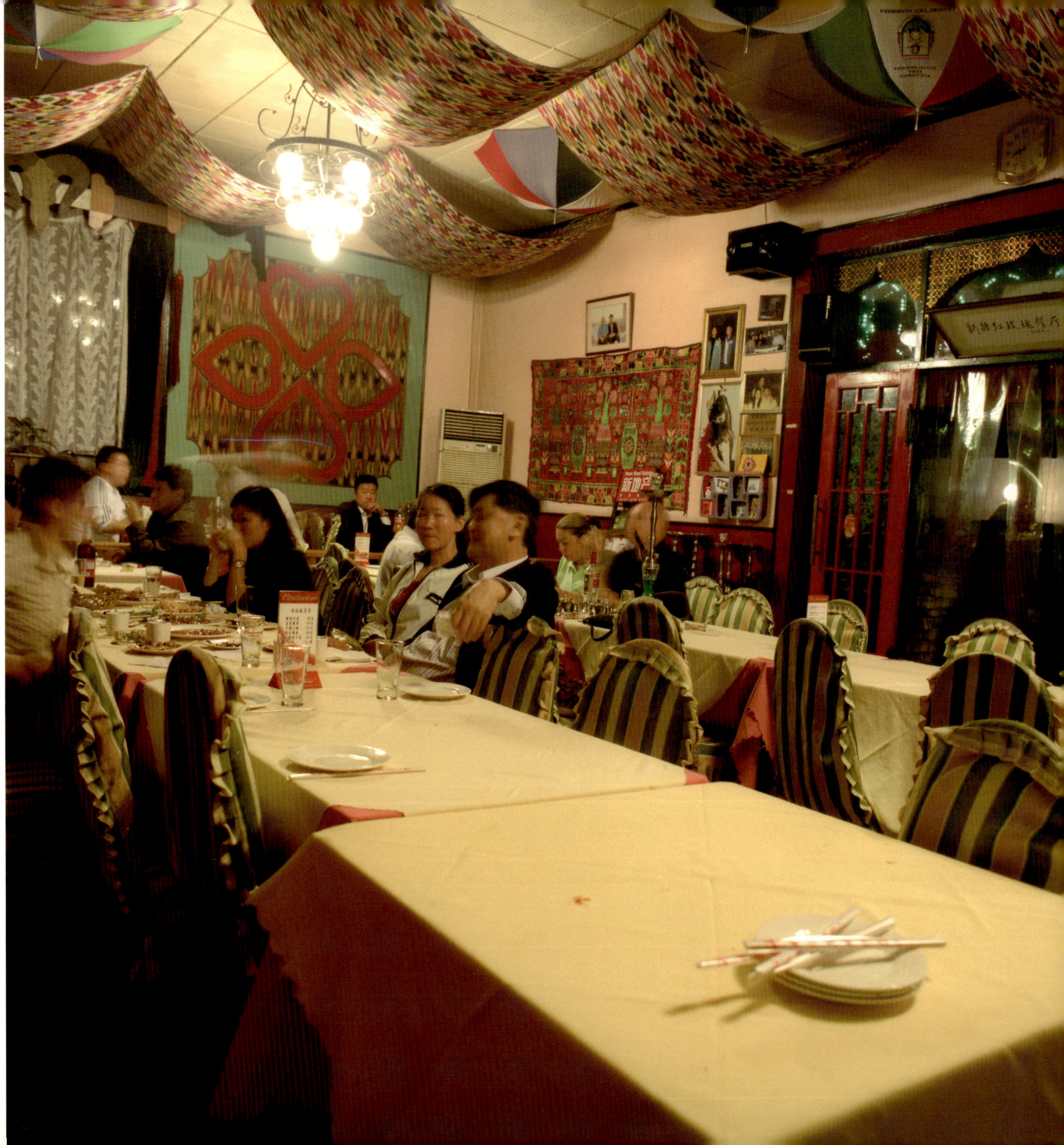

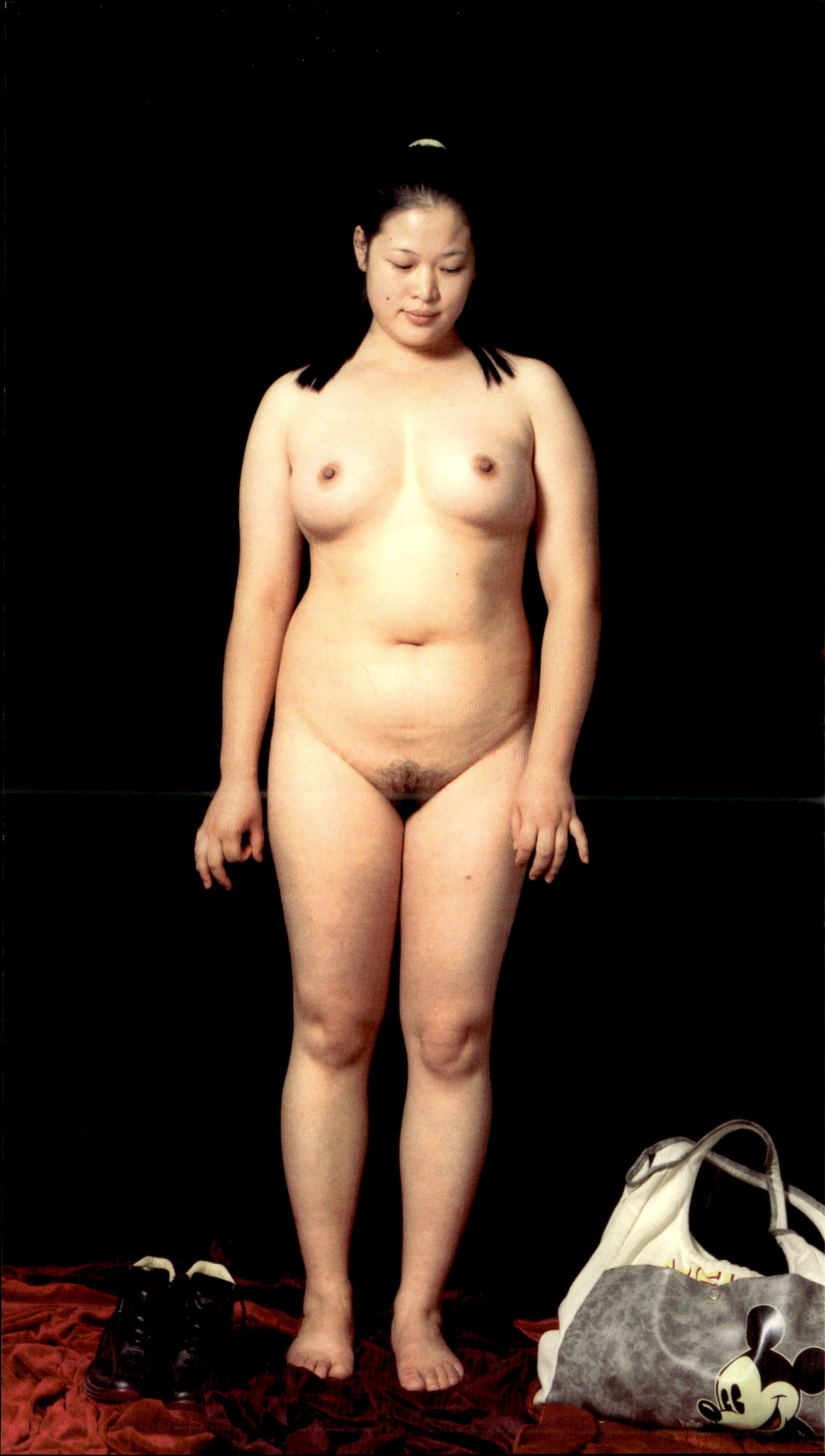

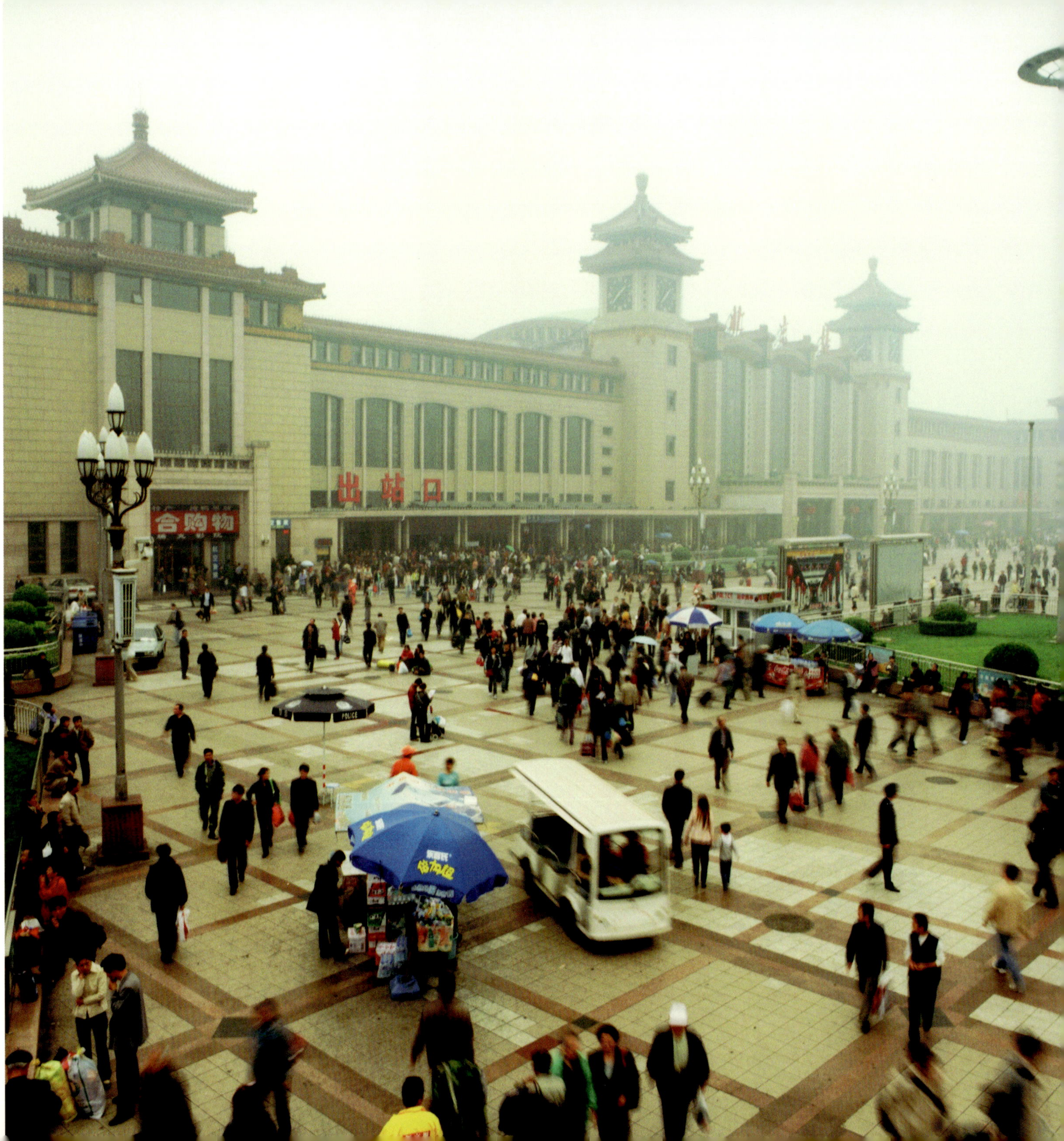
出站口
POLICE

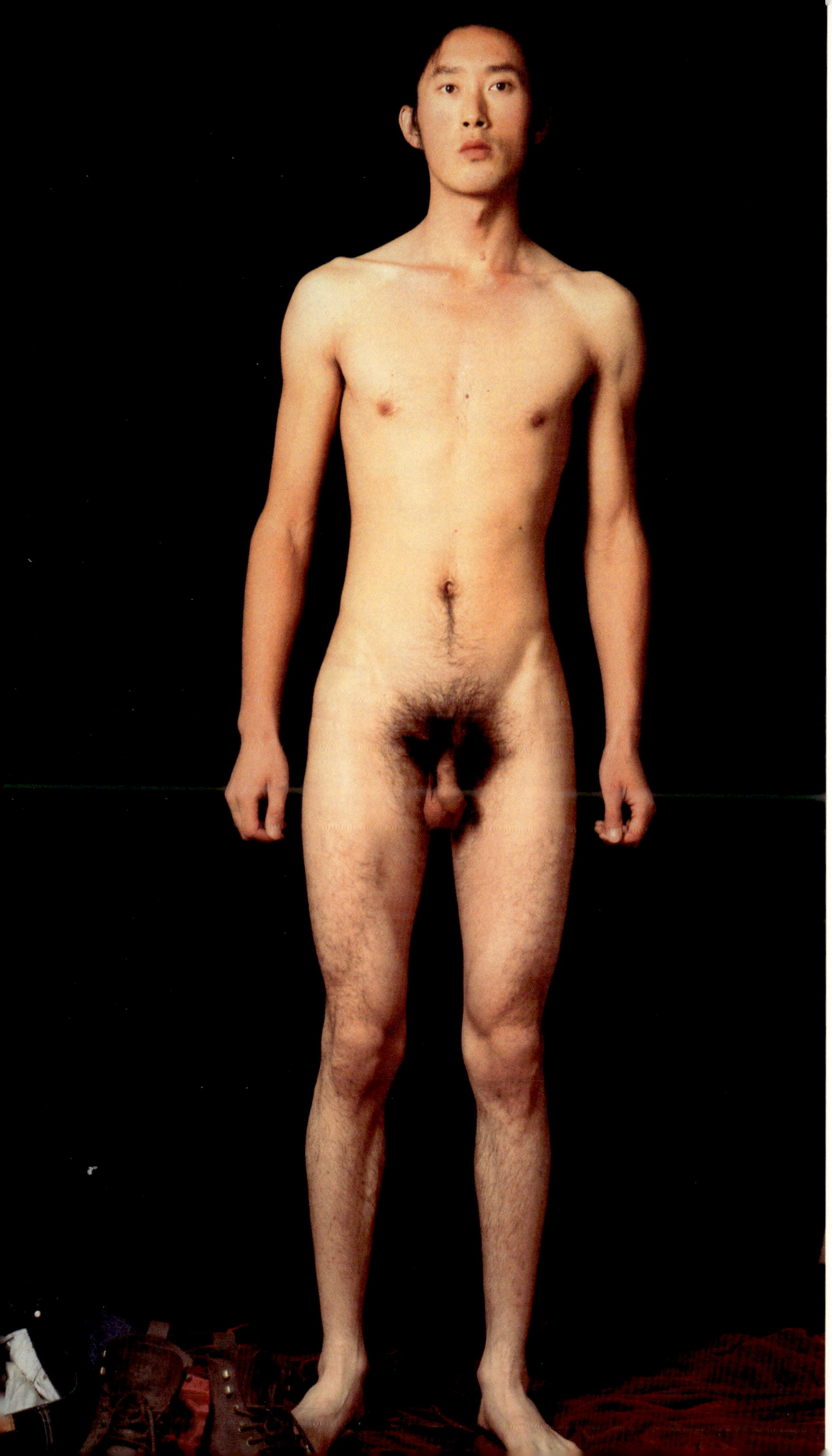

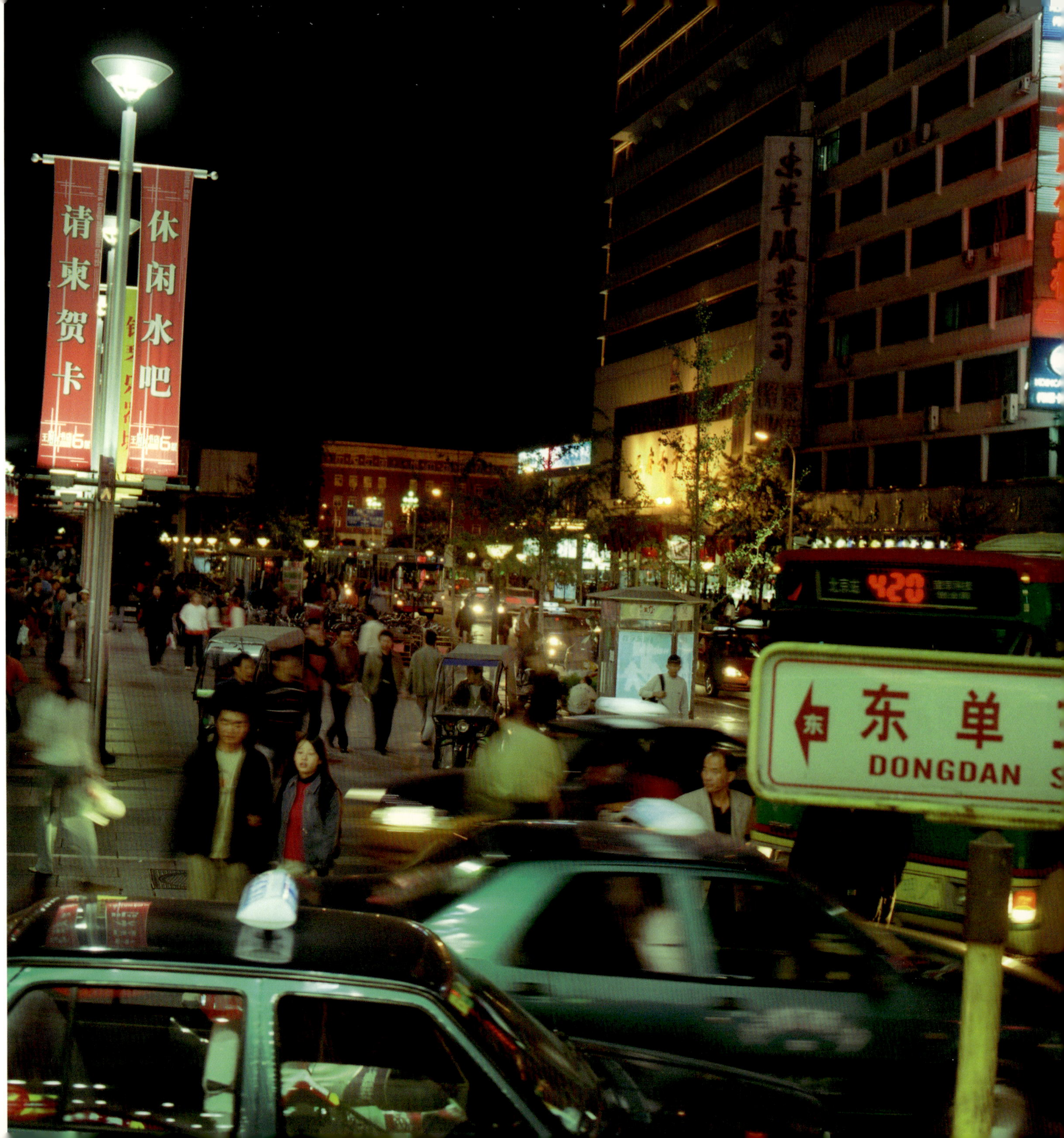
请柬贺卡
休闲水吧
东单
DONGDAN
420

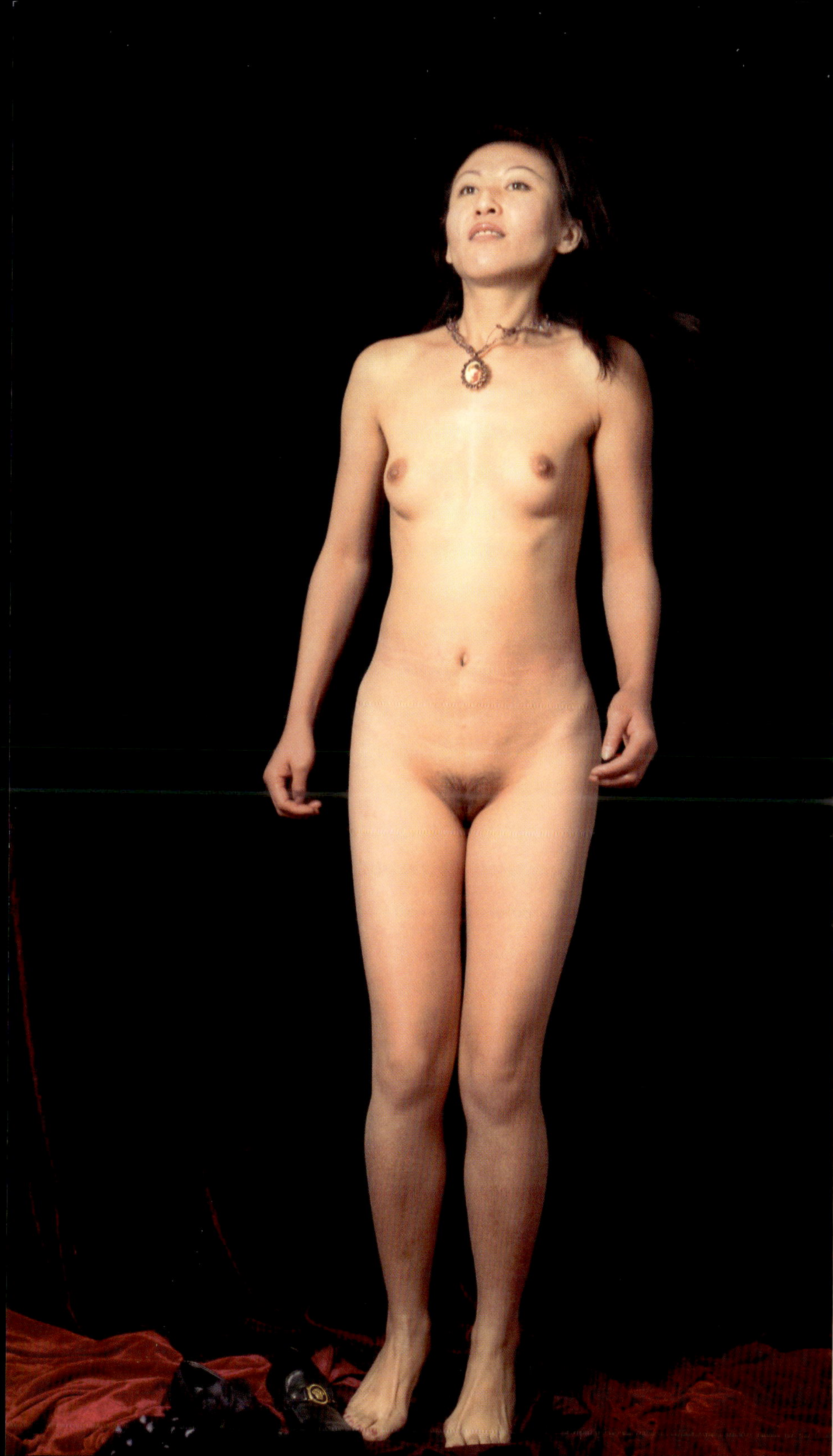

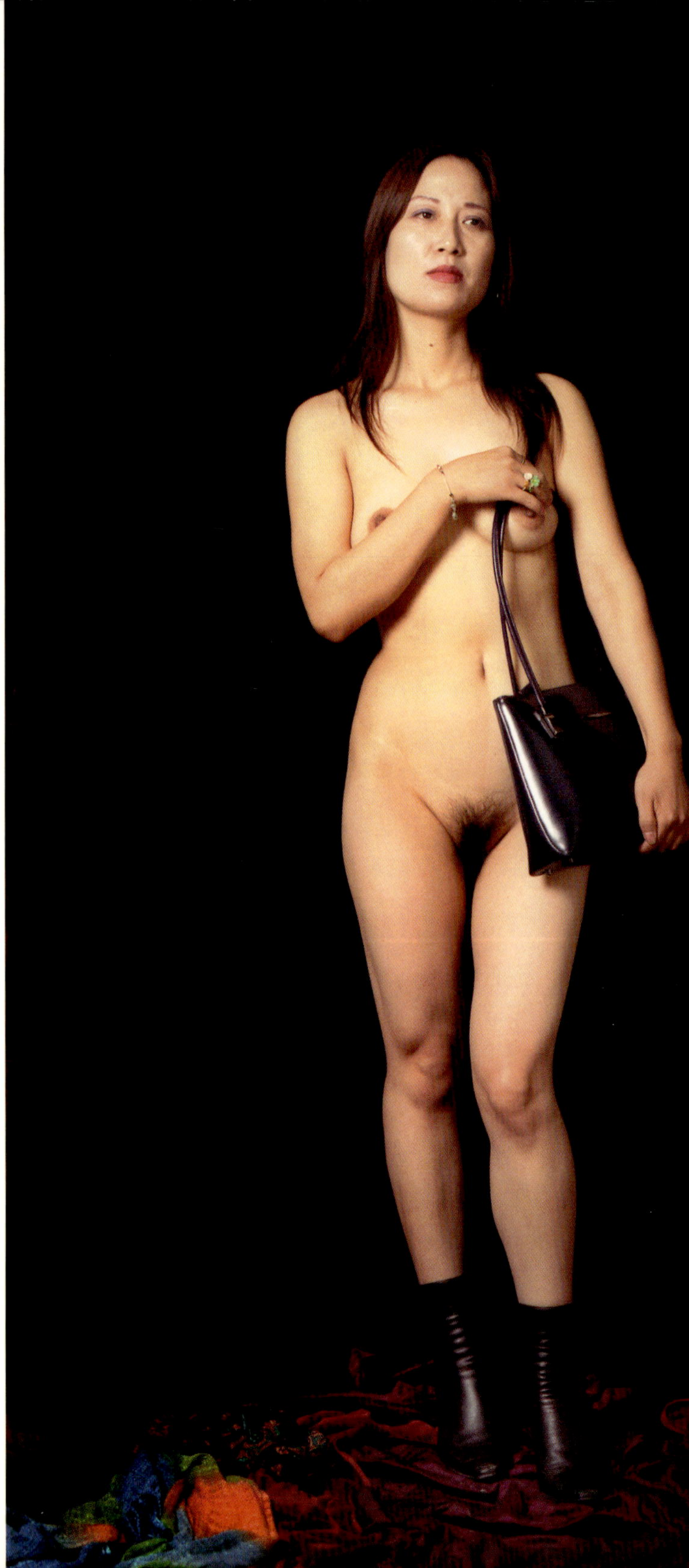

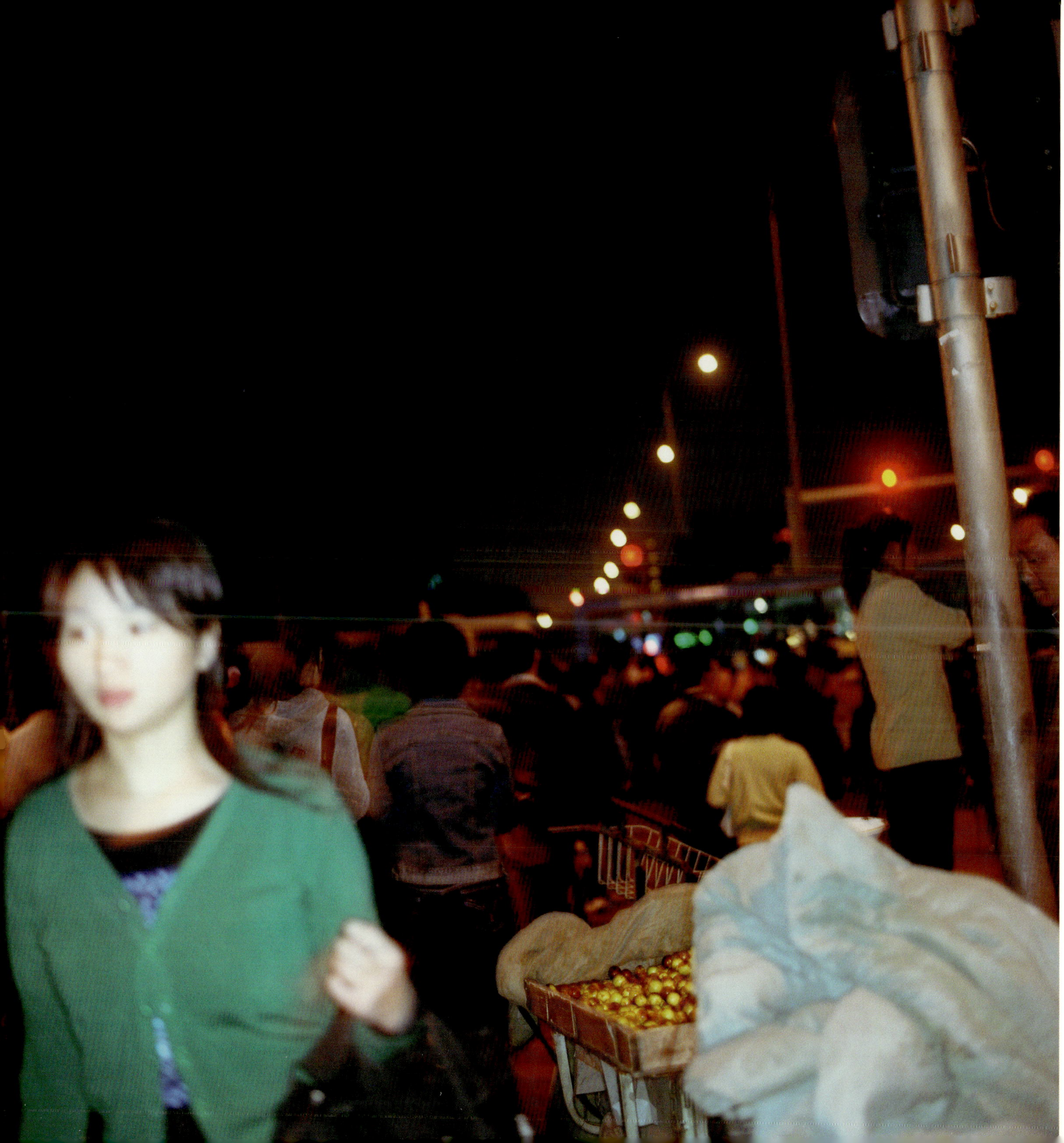

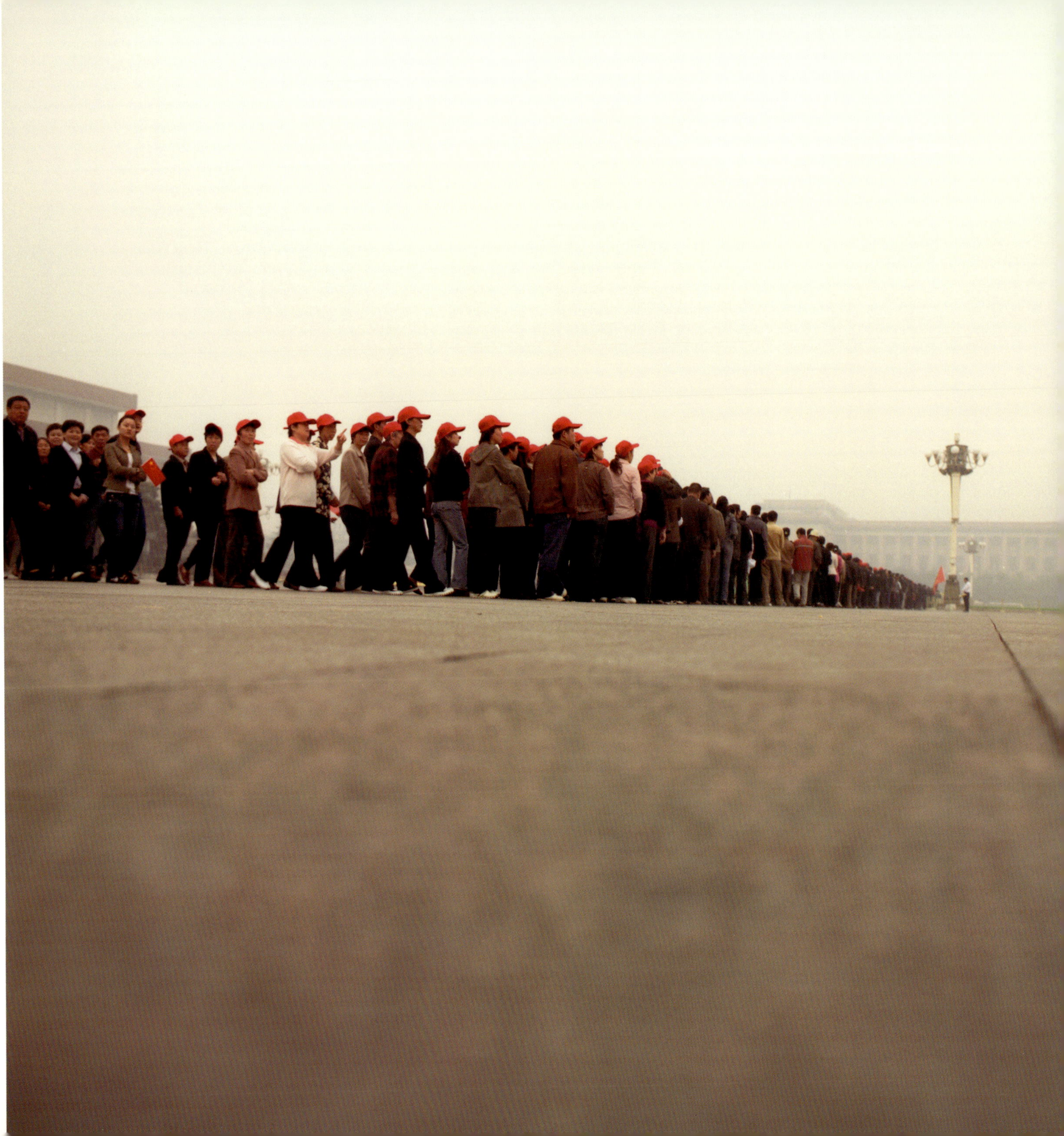

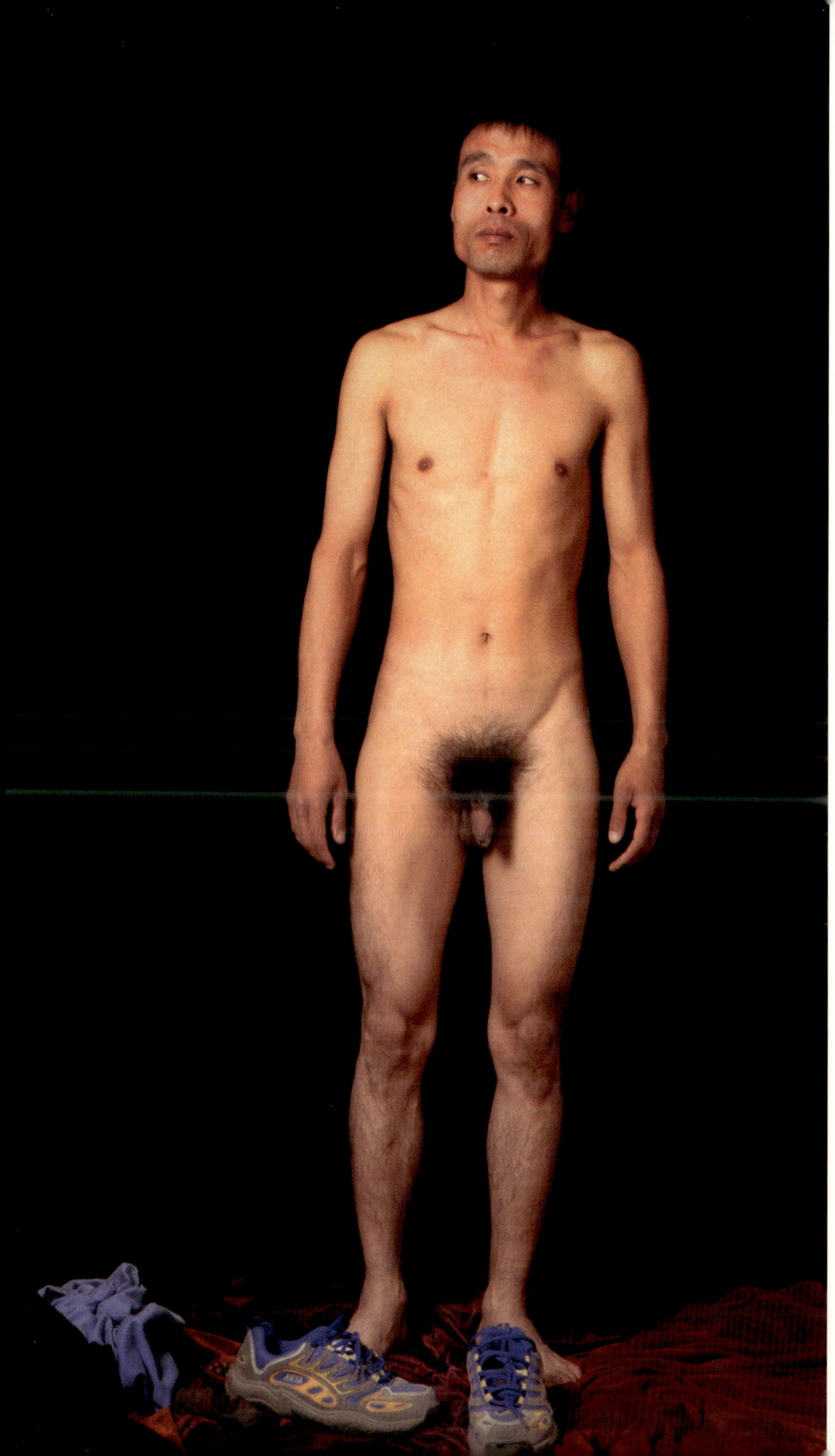

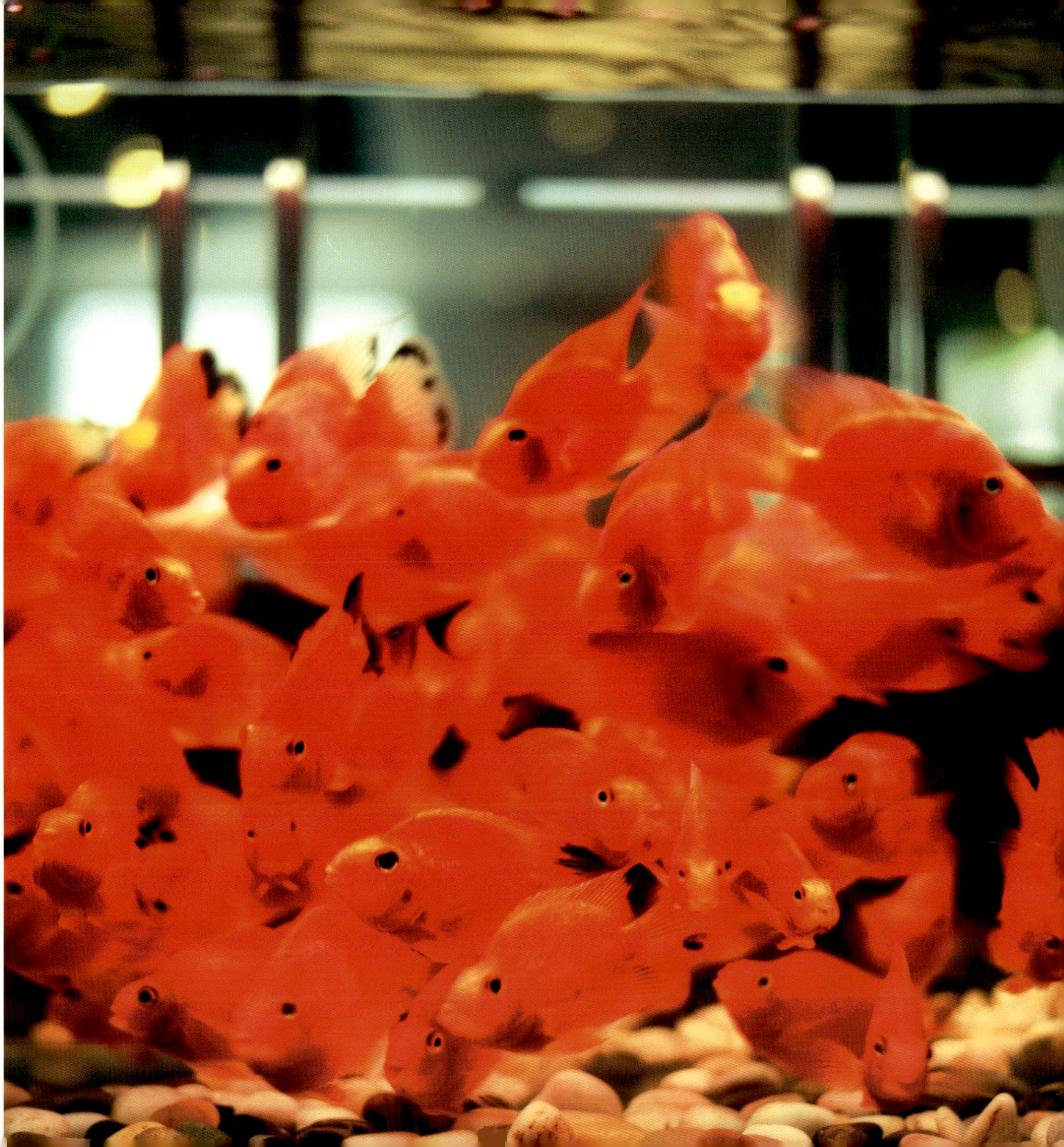

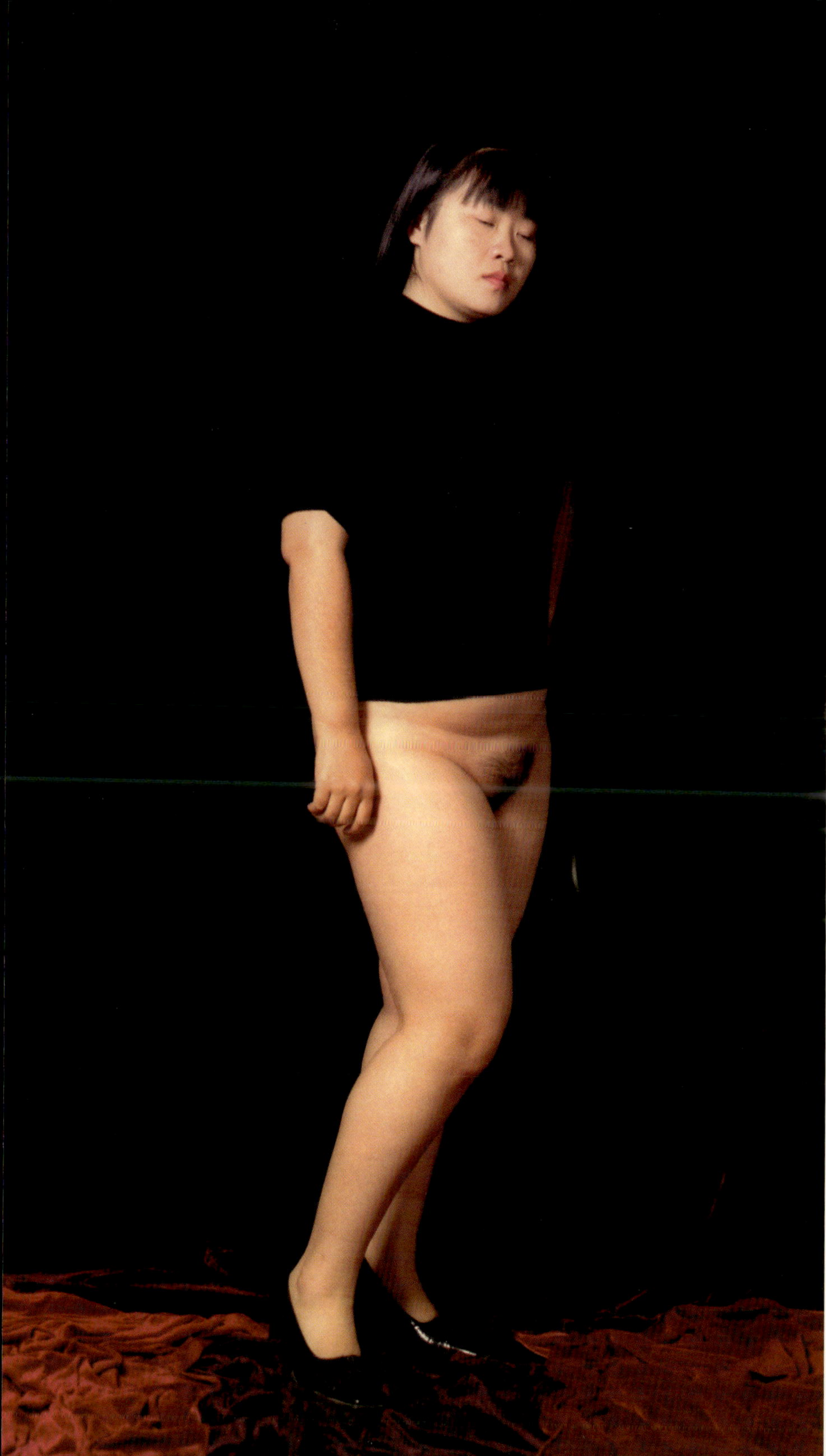

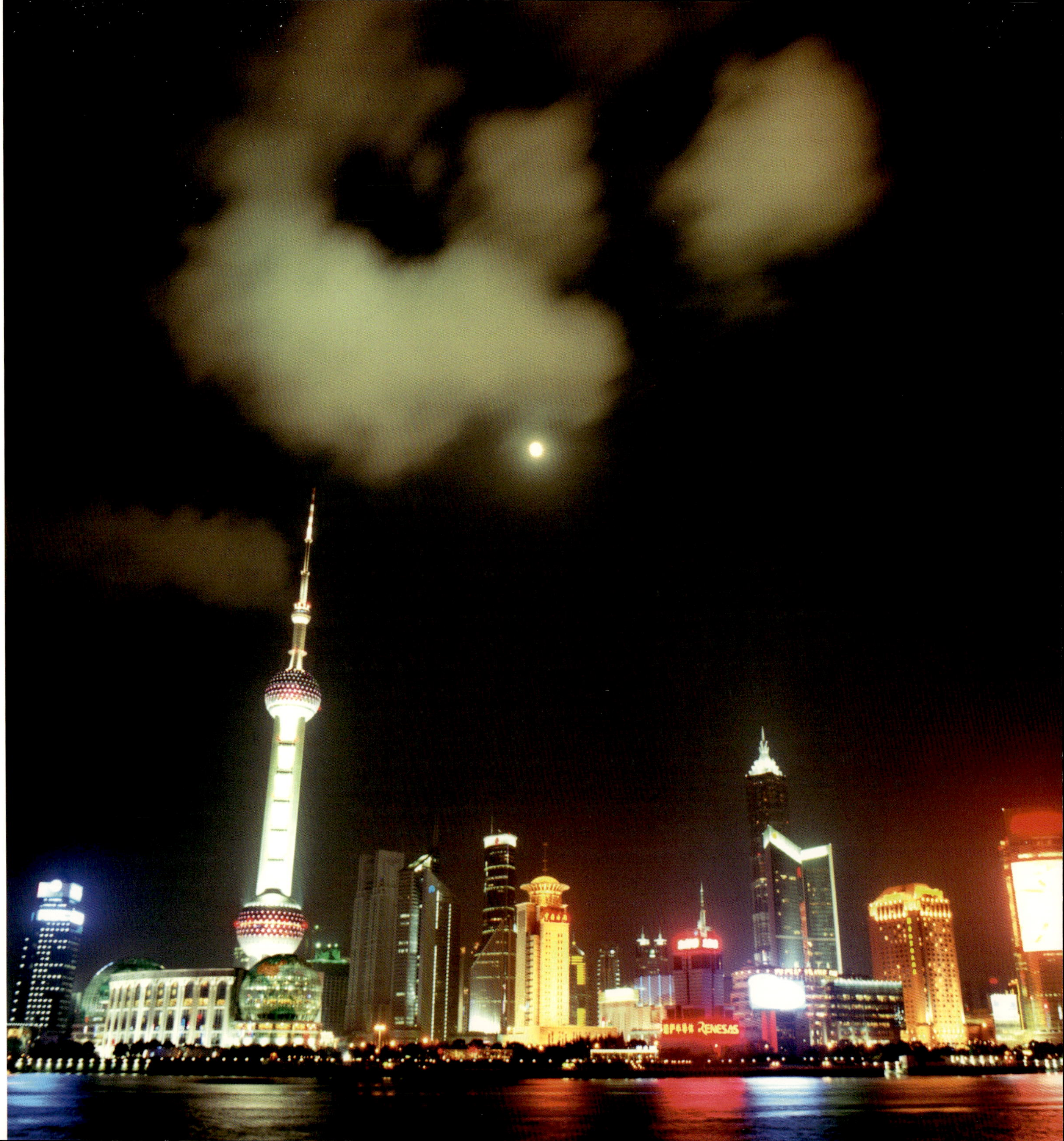
RENESAS

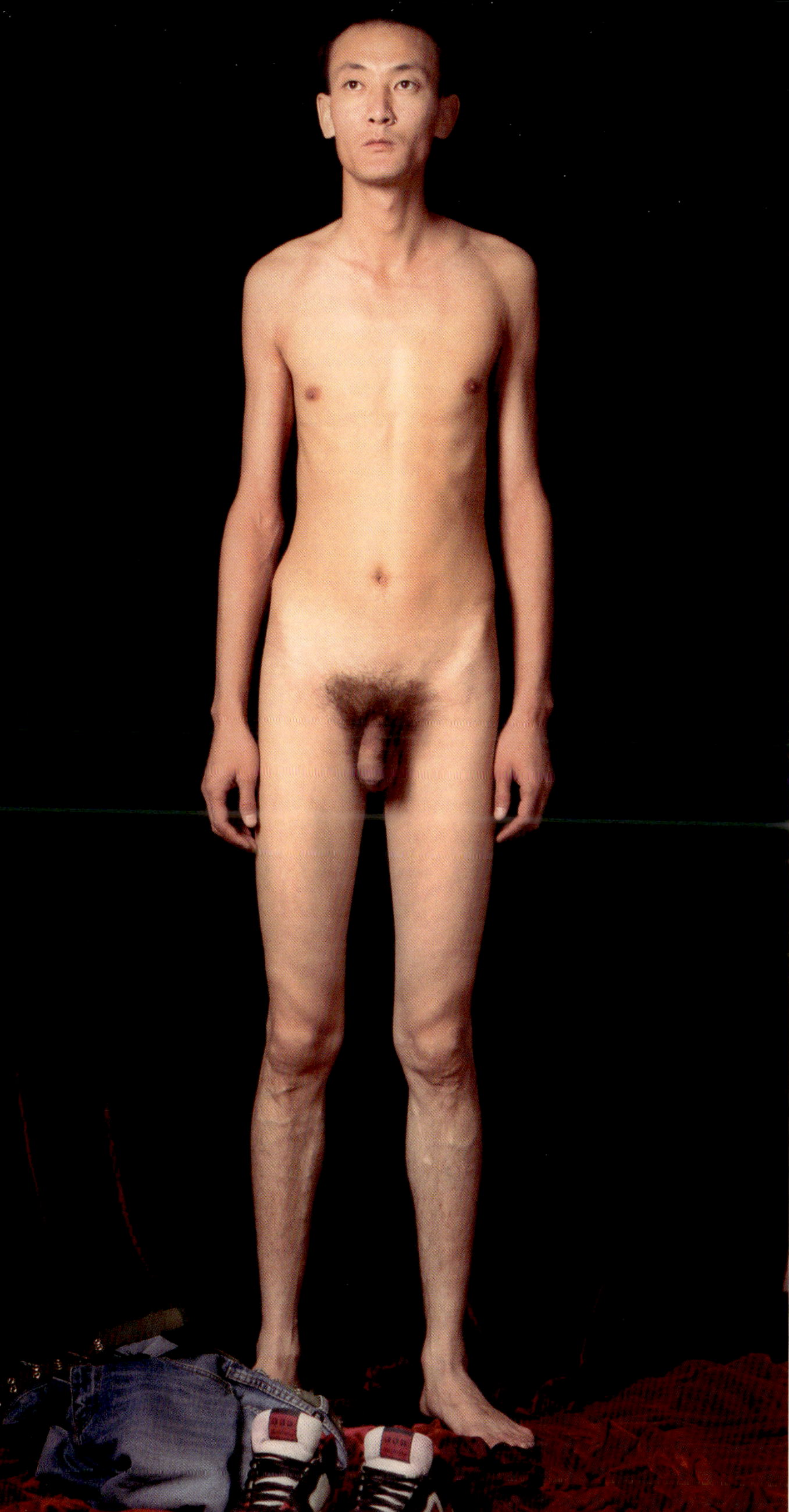

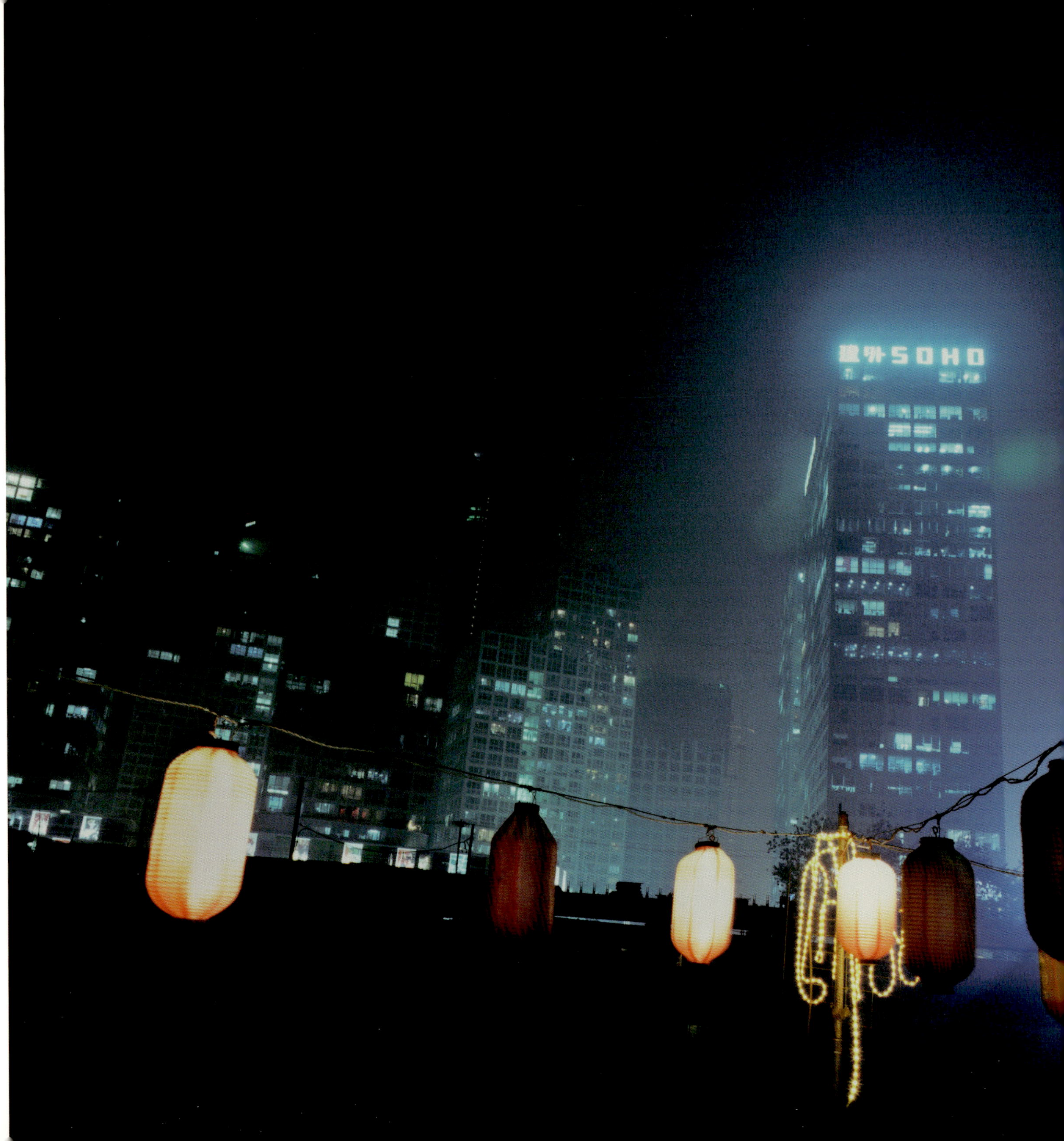
建外SOHO

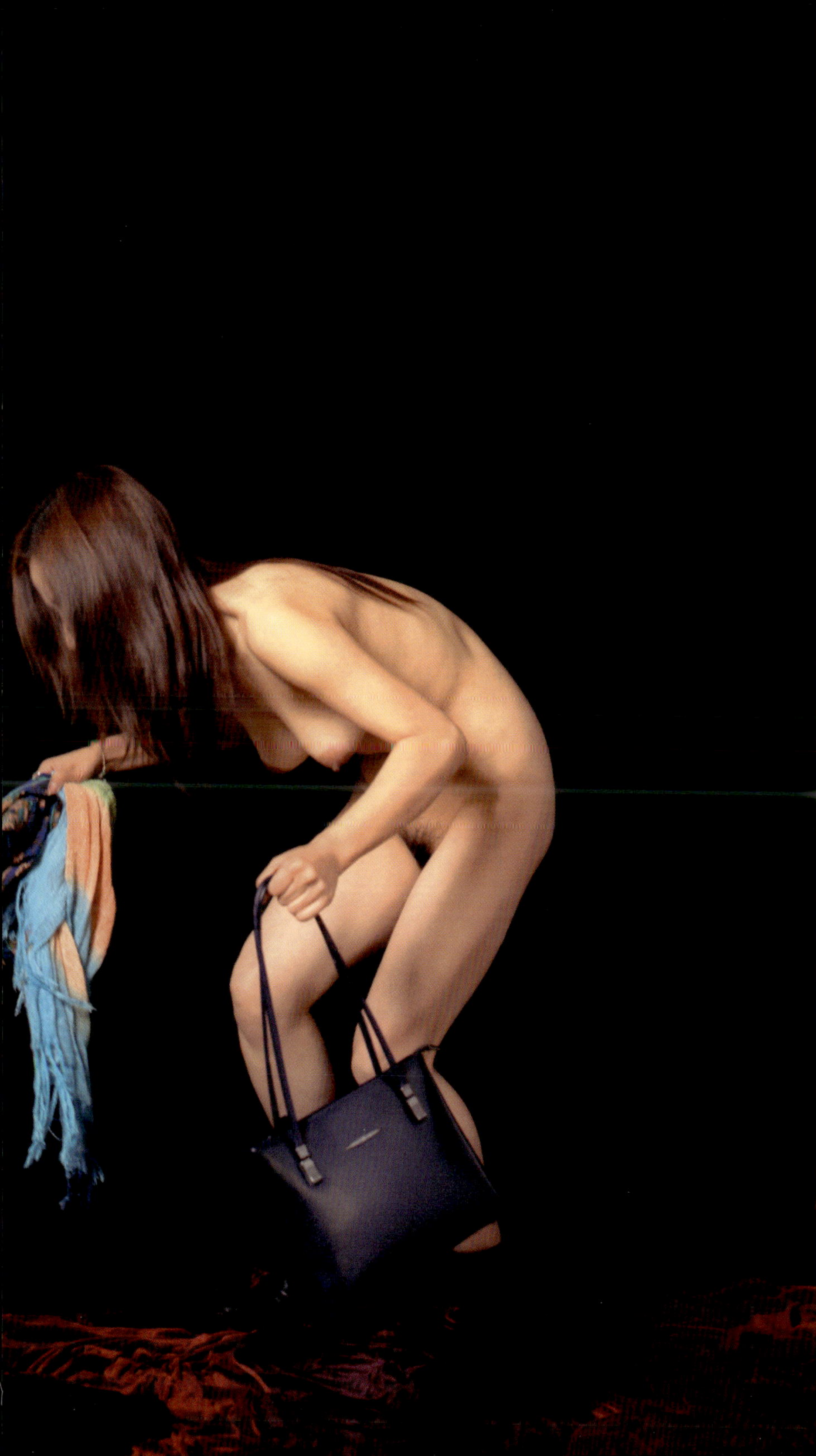

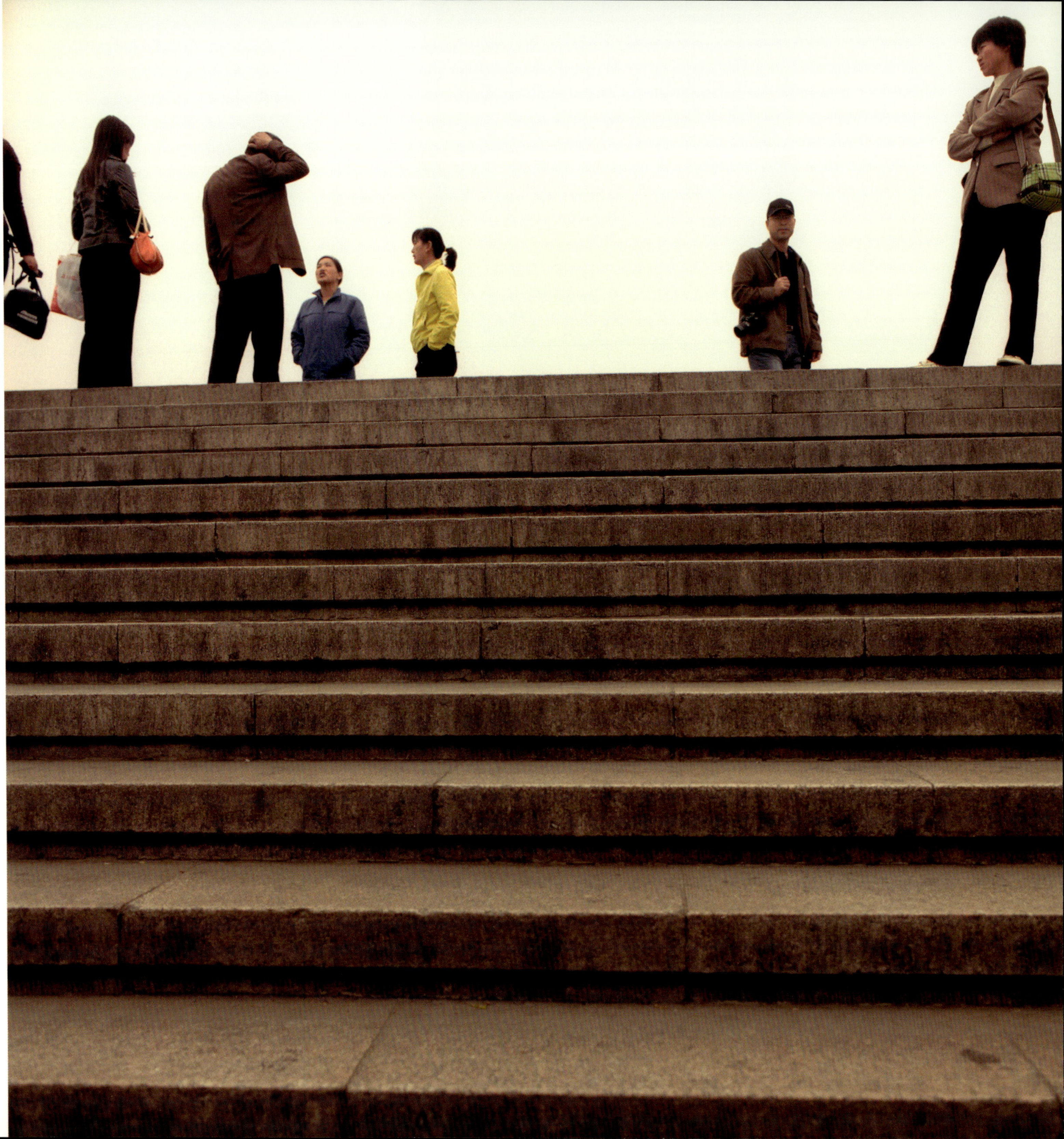

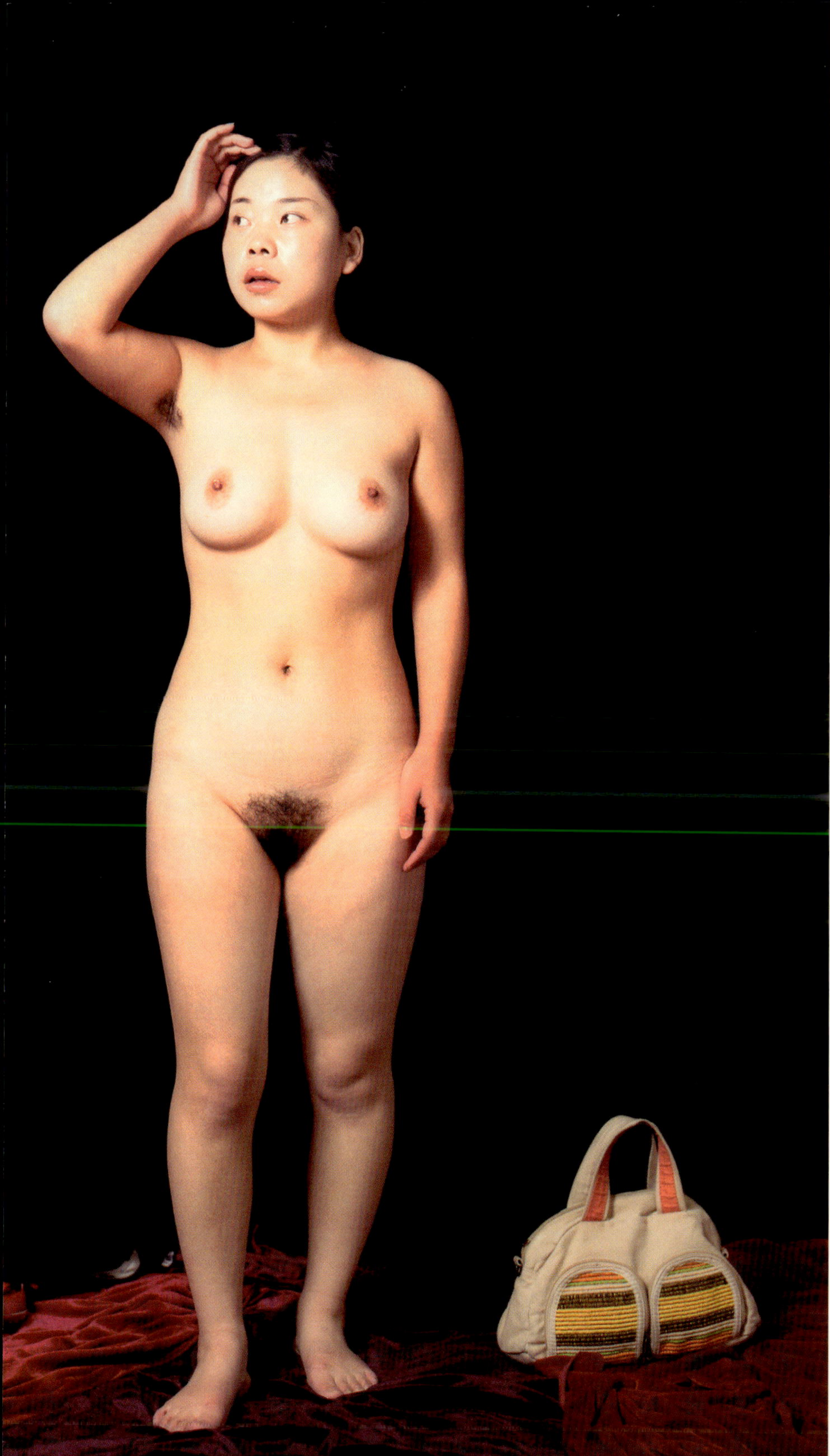

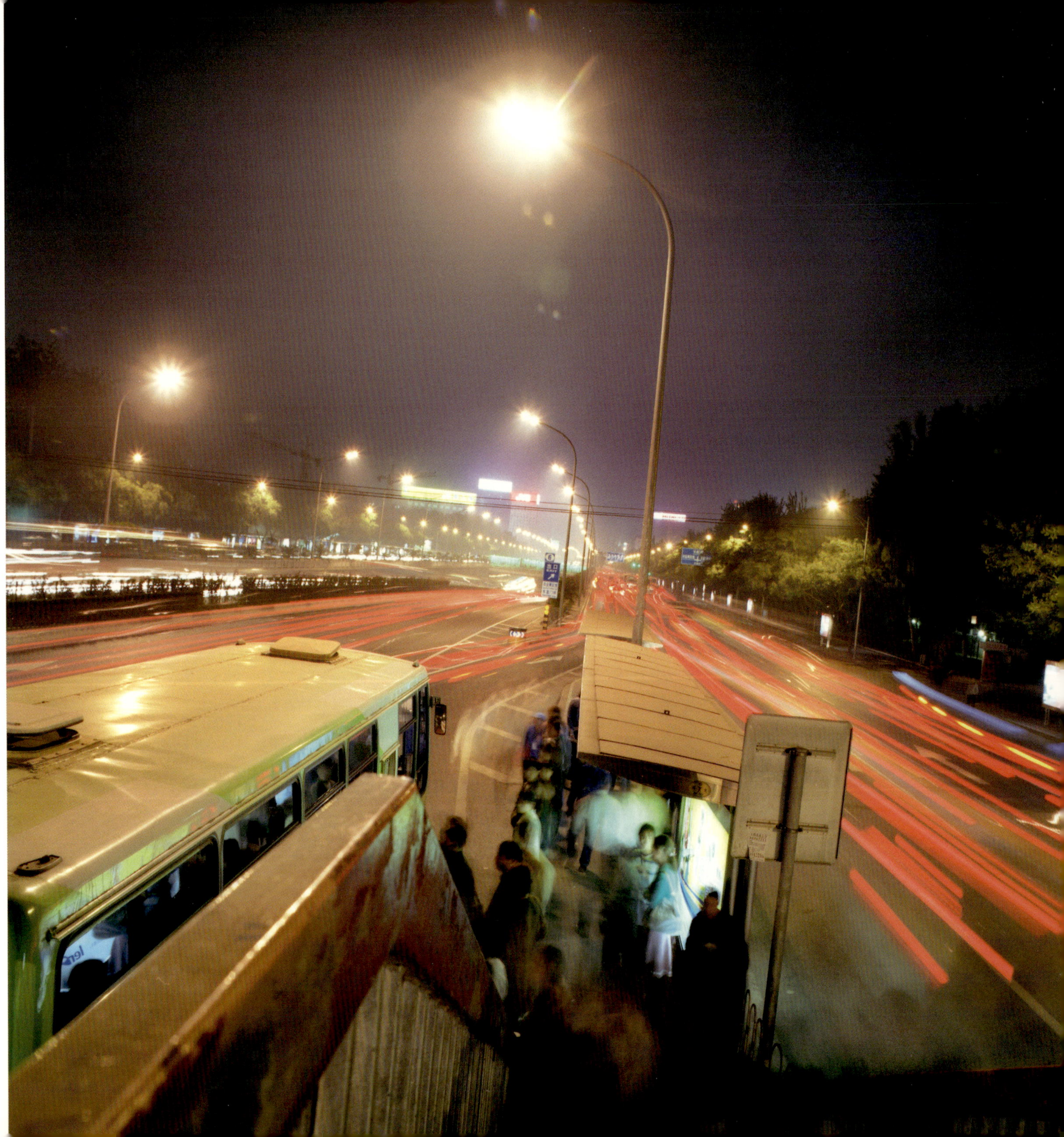

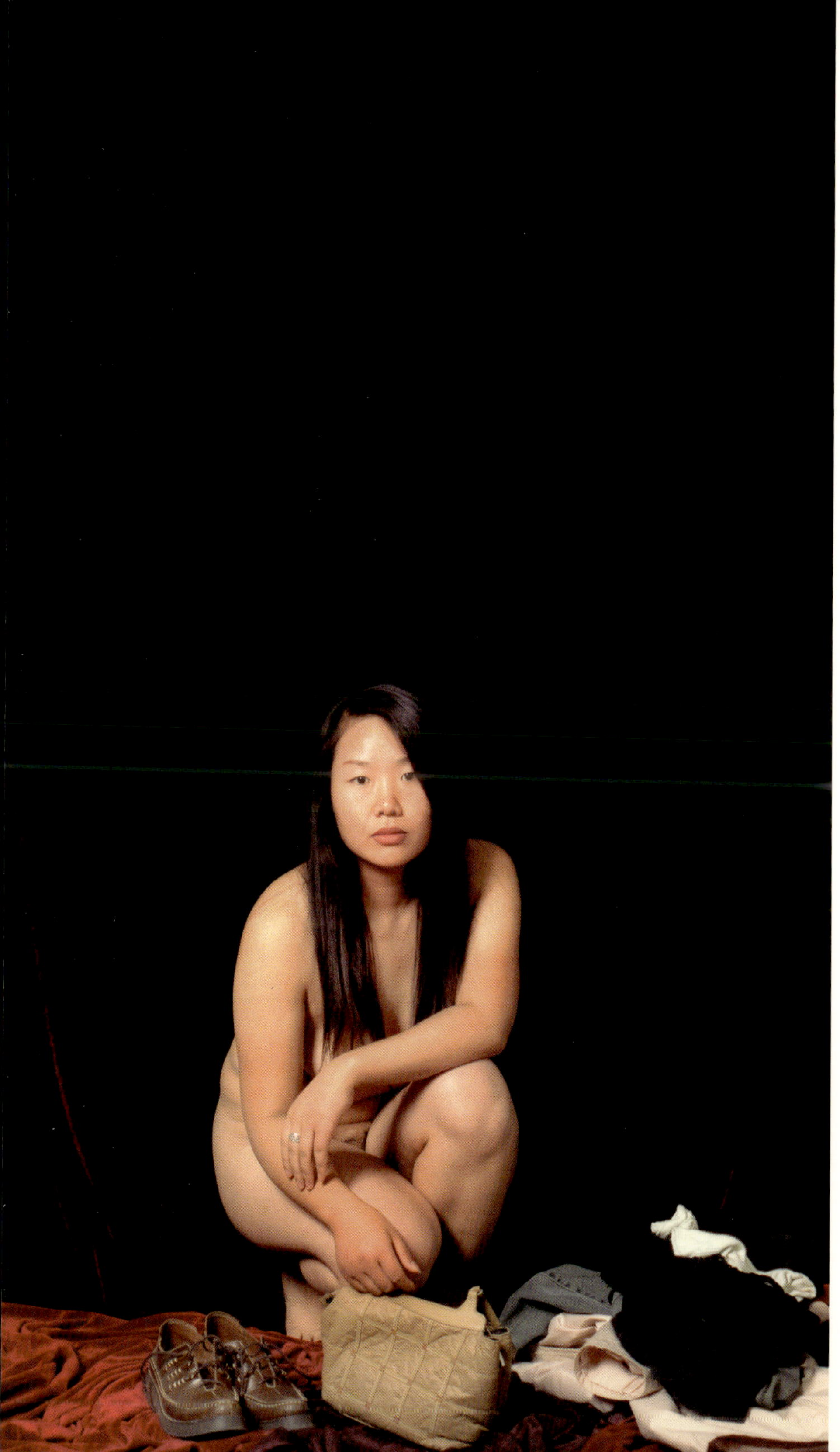

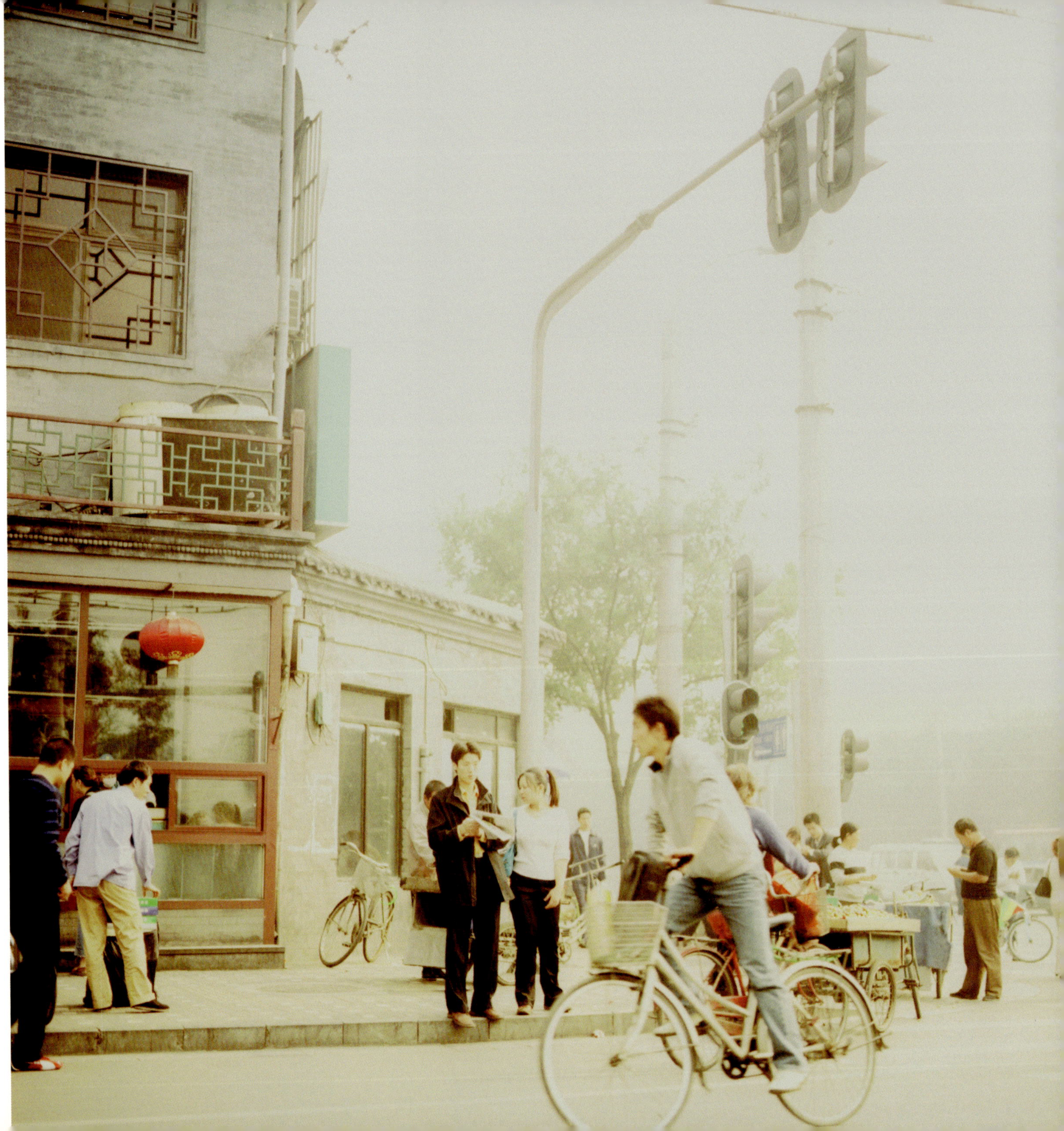

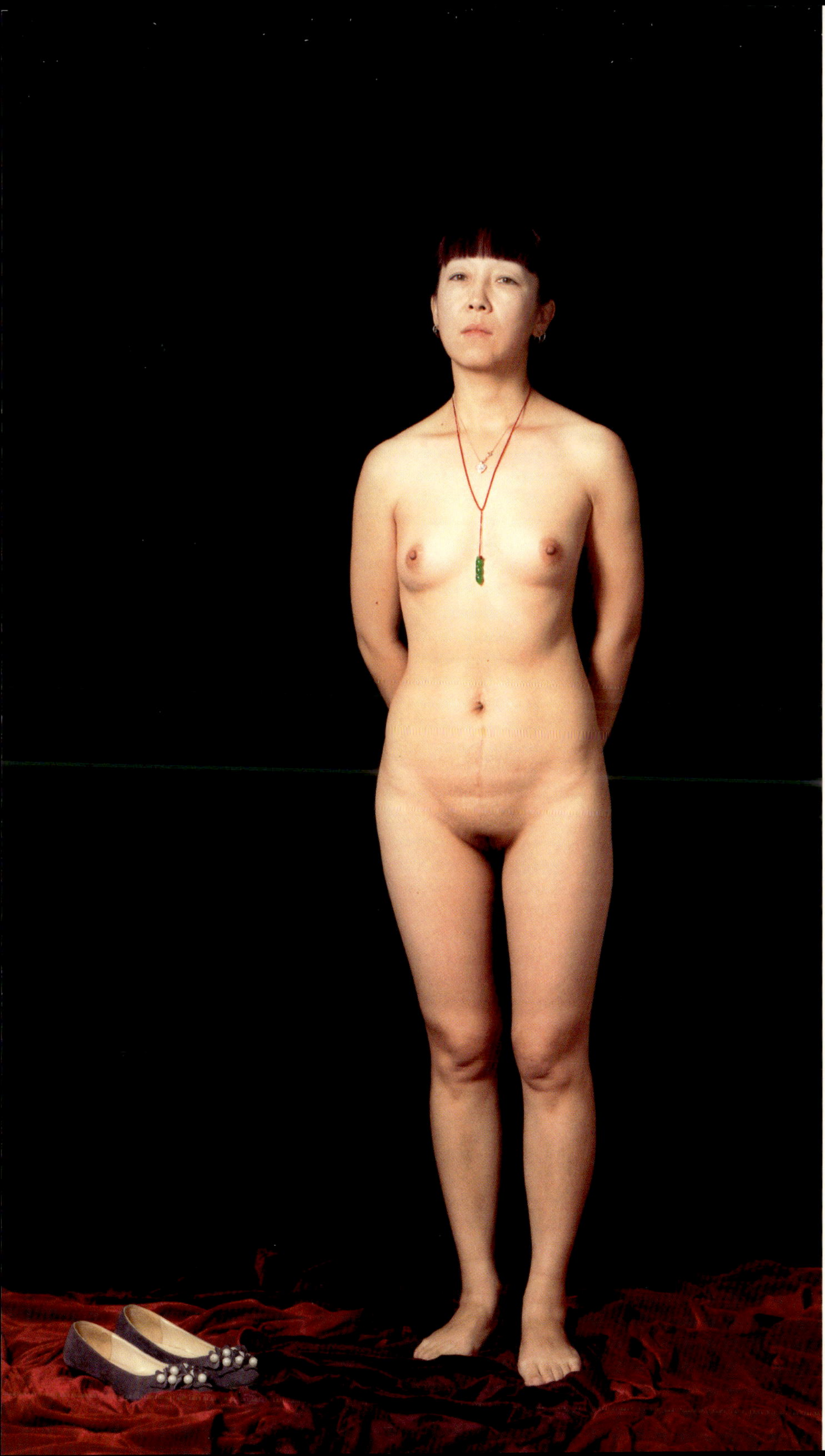

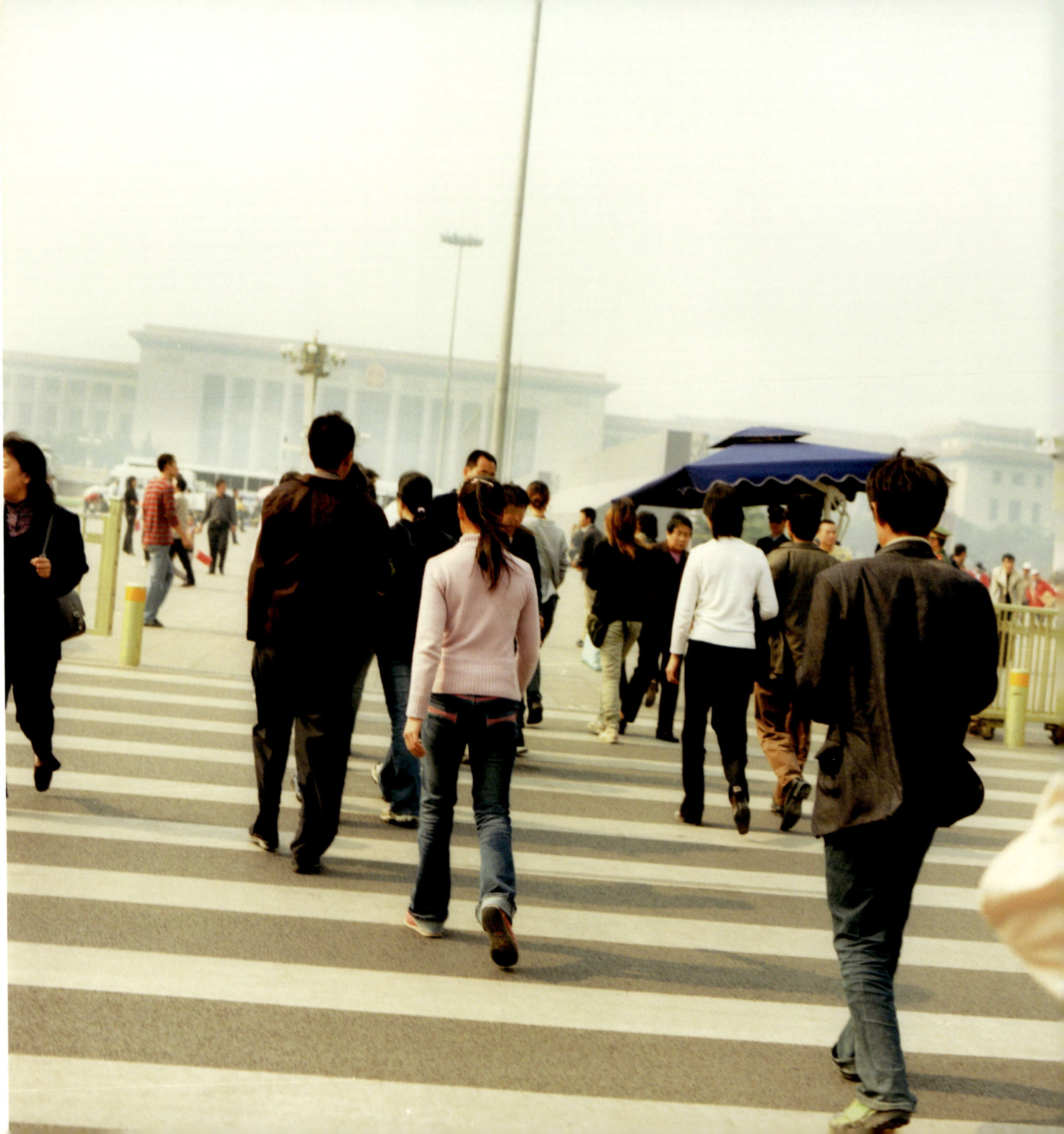

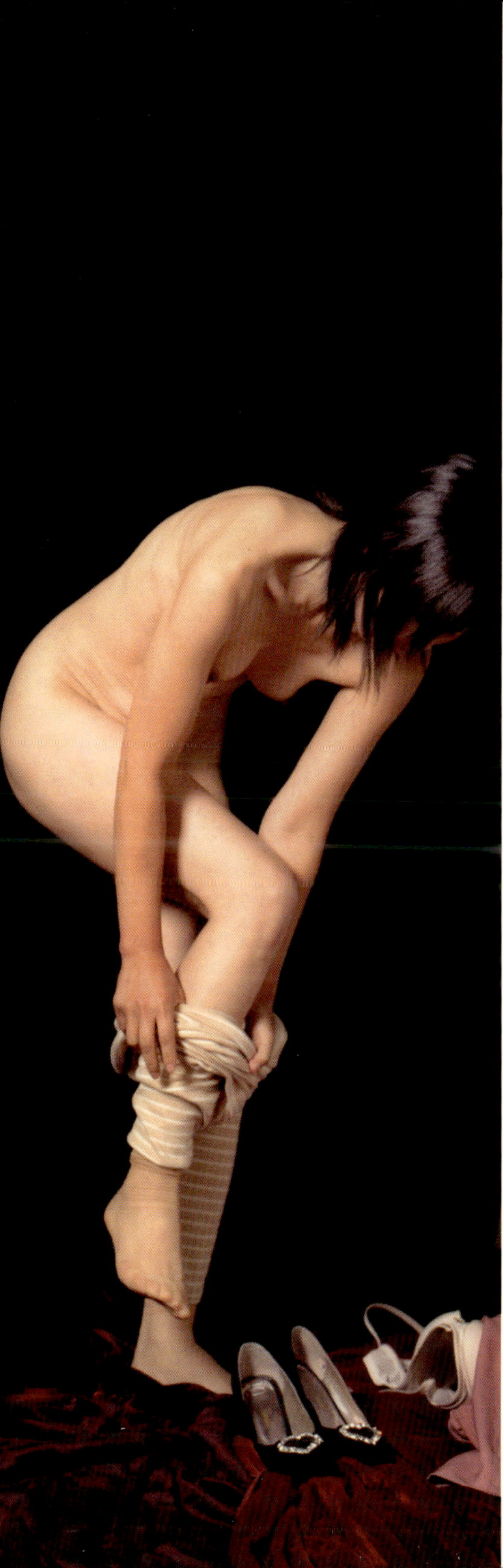

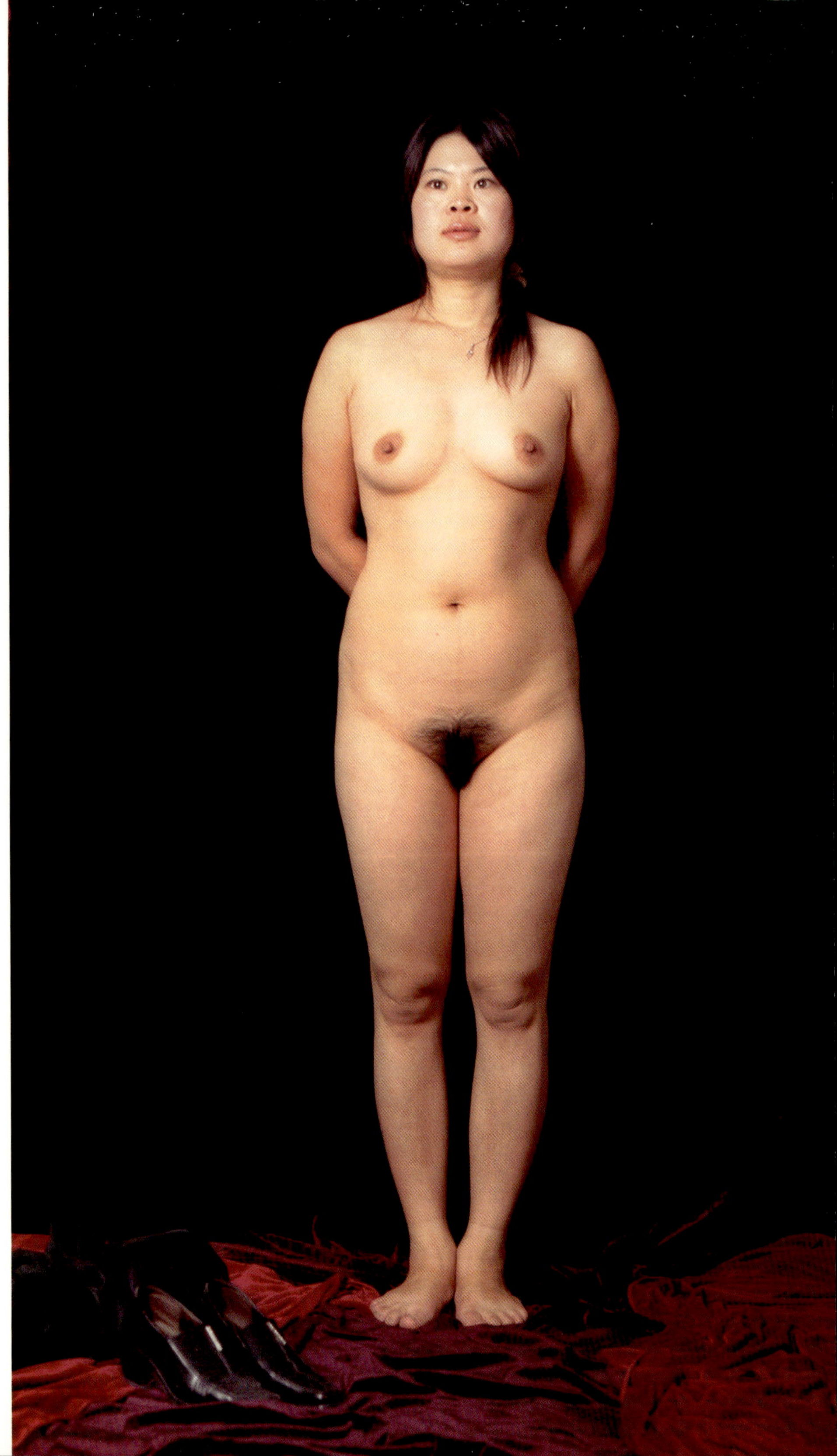

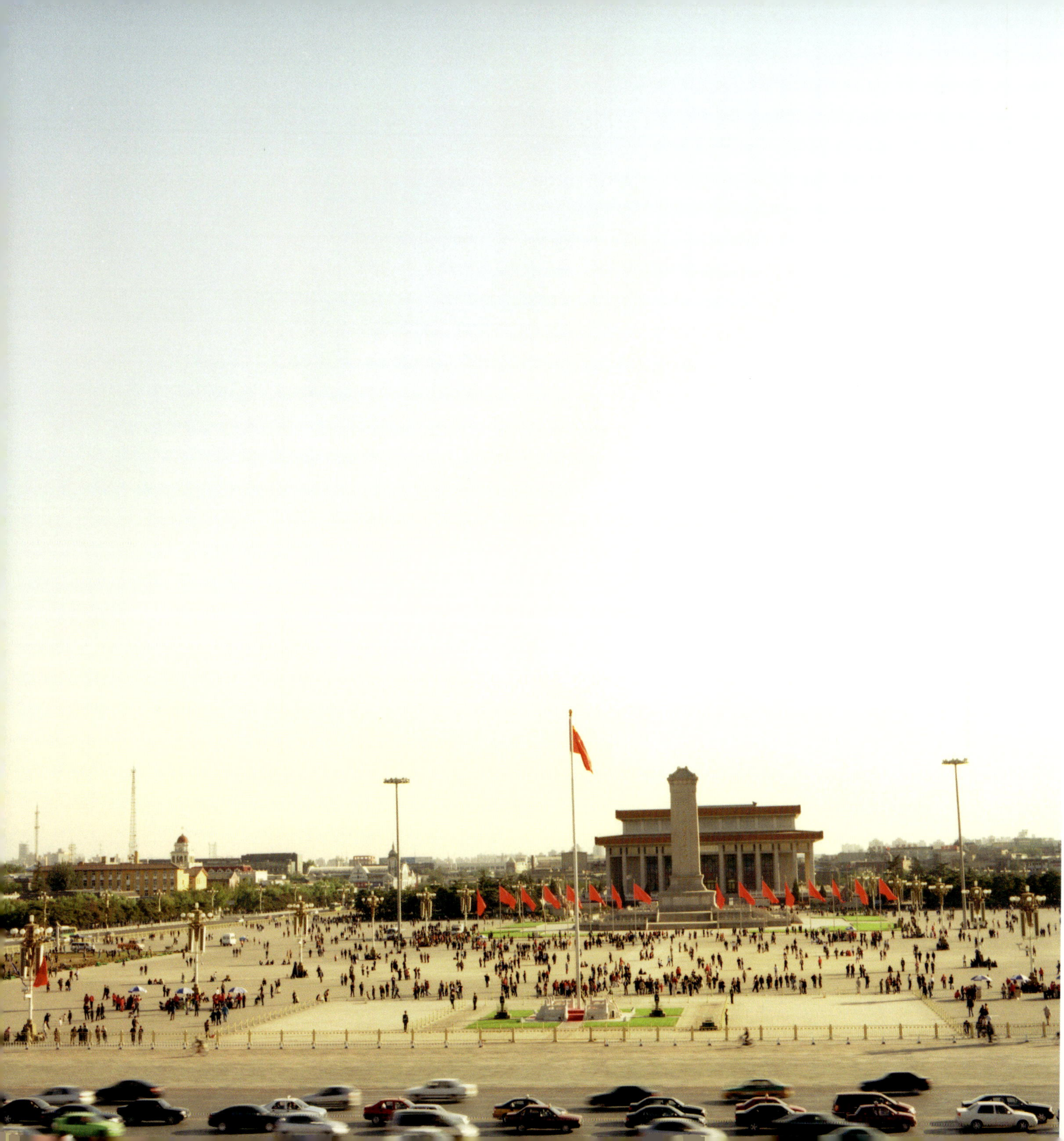

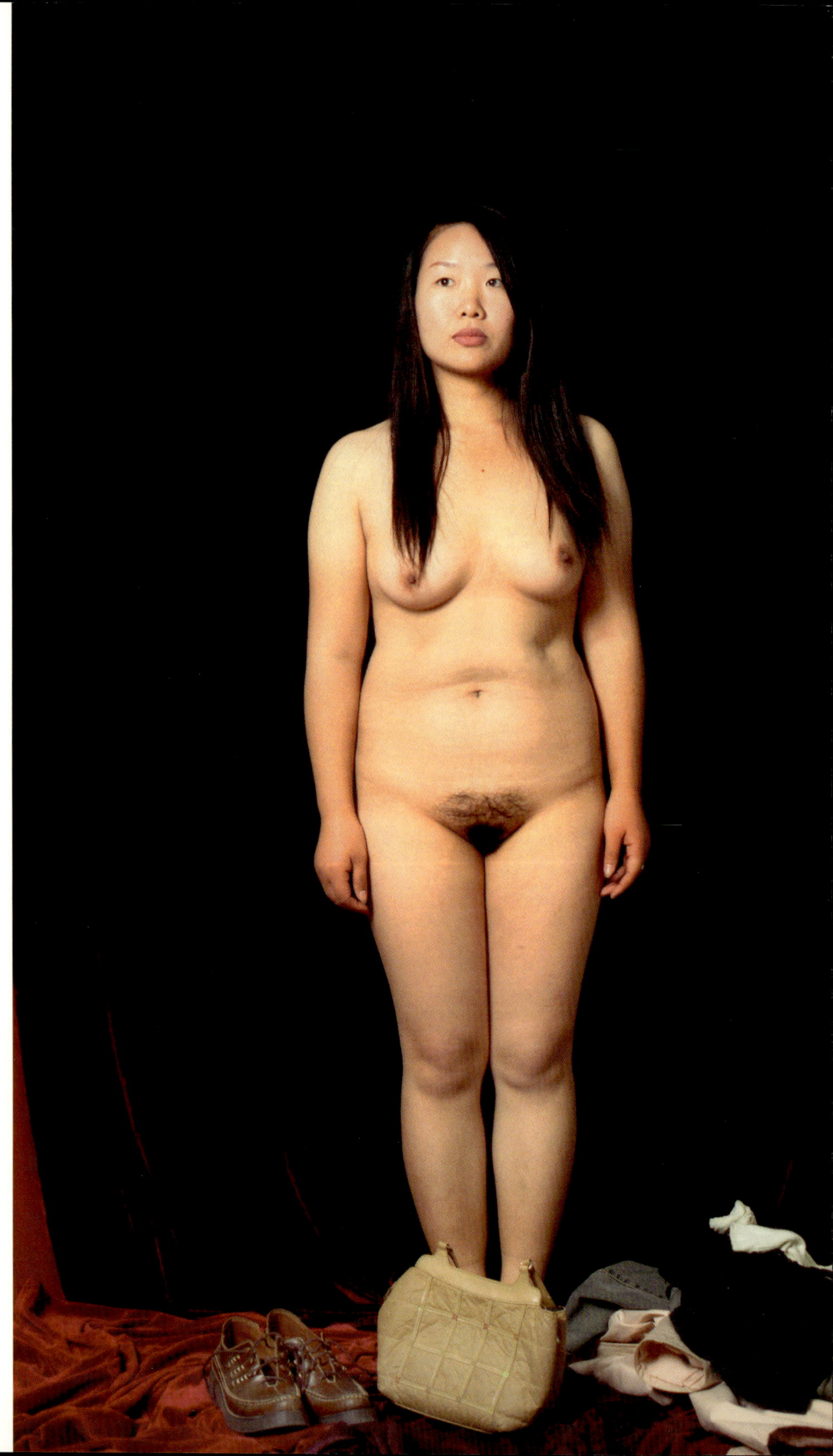

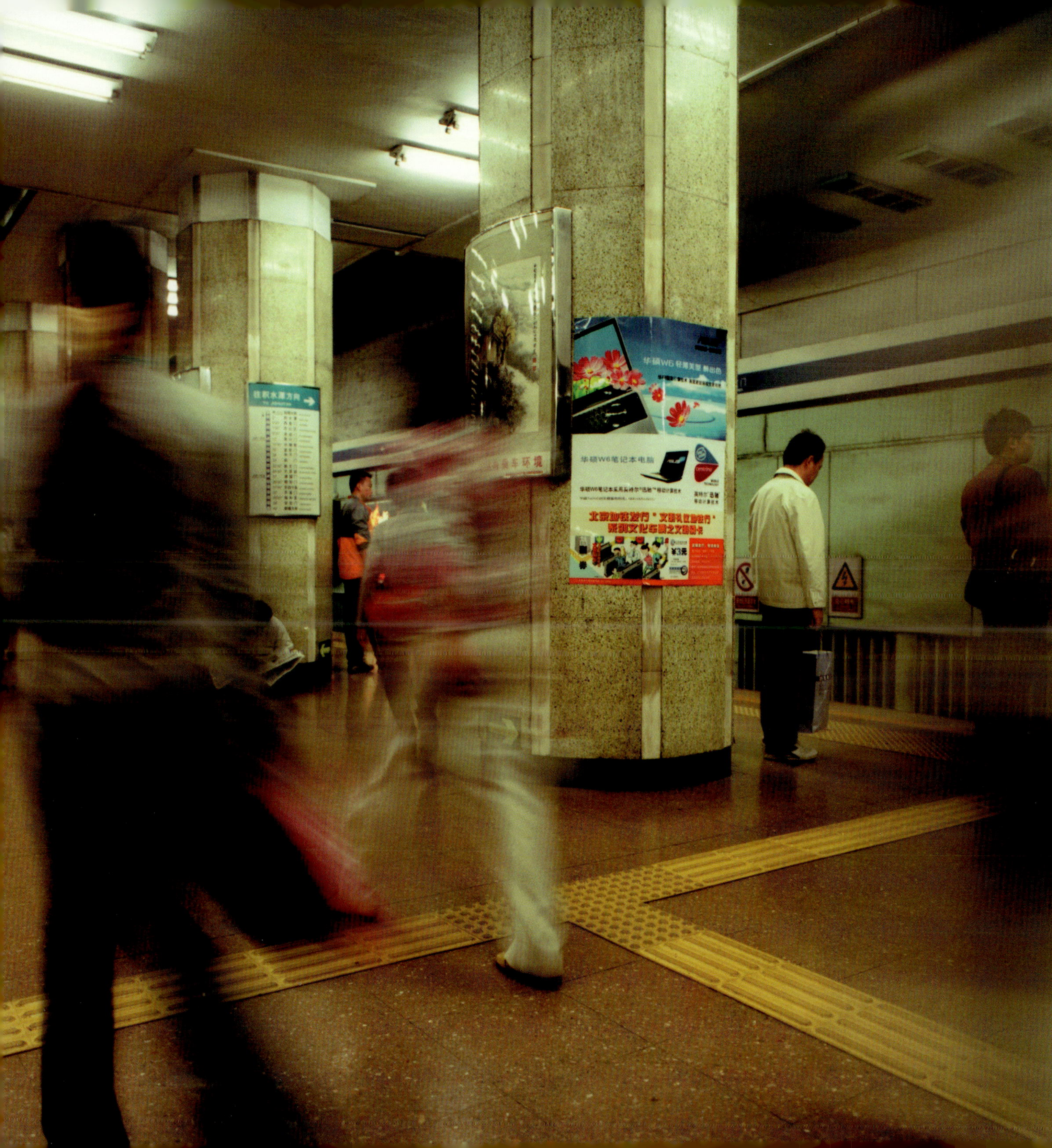
华硕W6笔记本电脑
¥3元

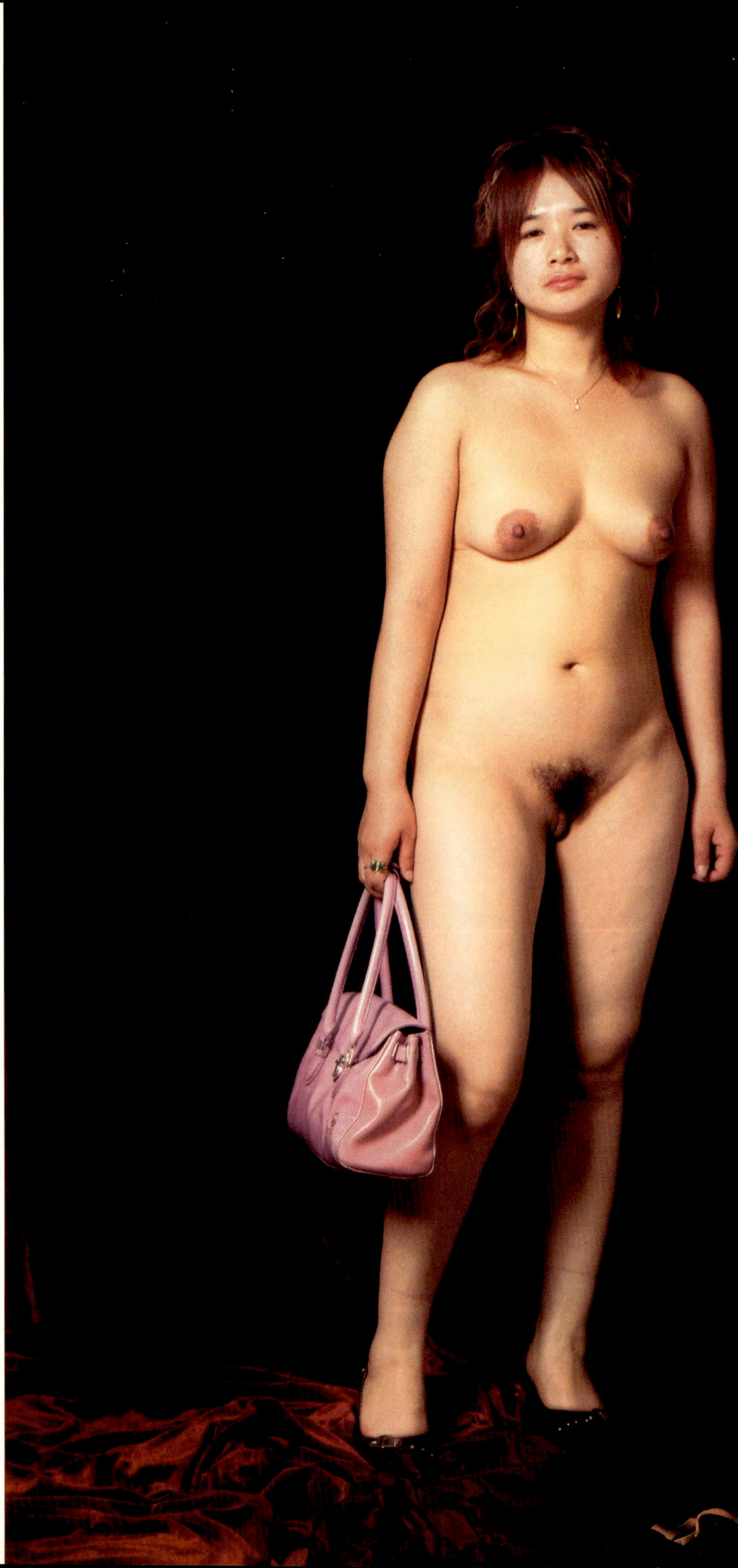

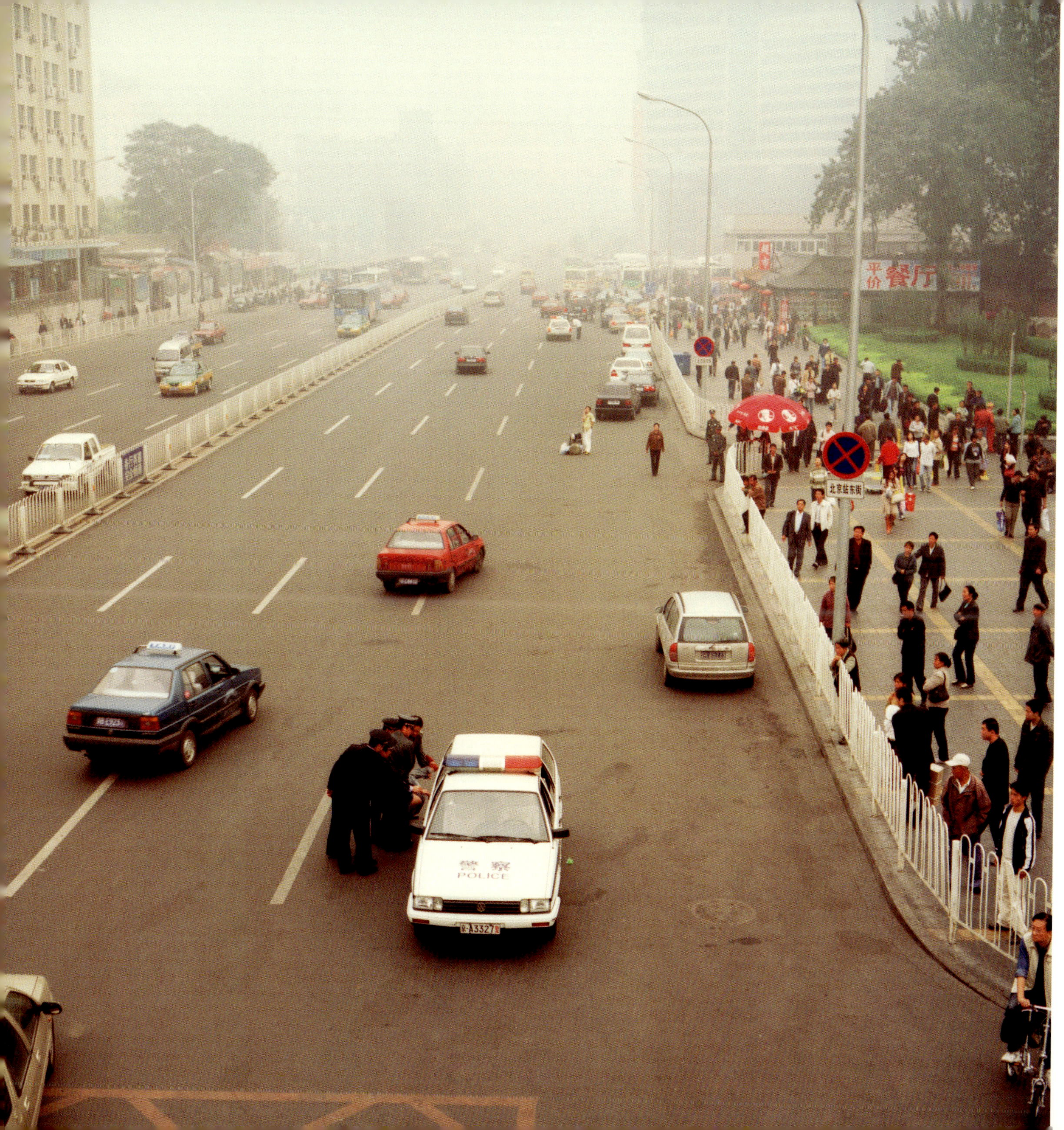
平价餐厅
警察
POLICE

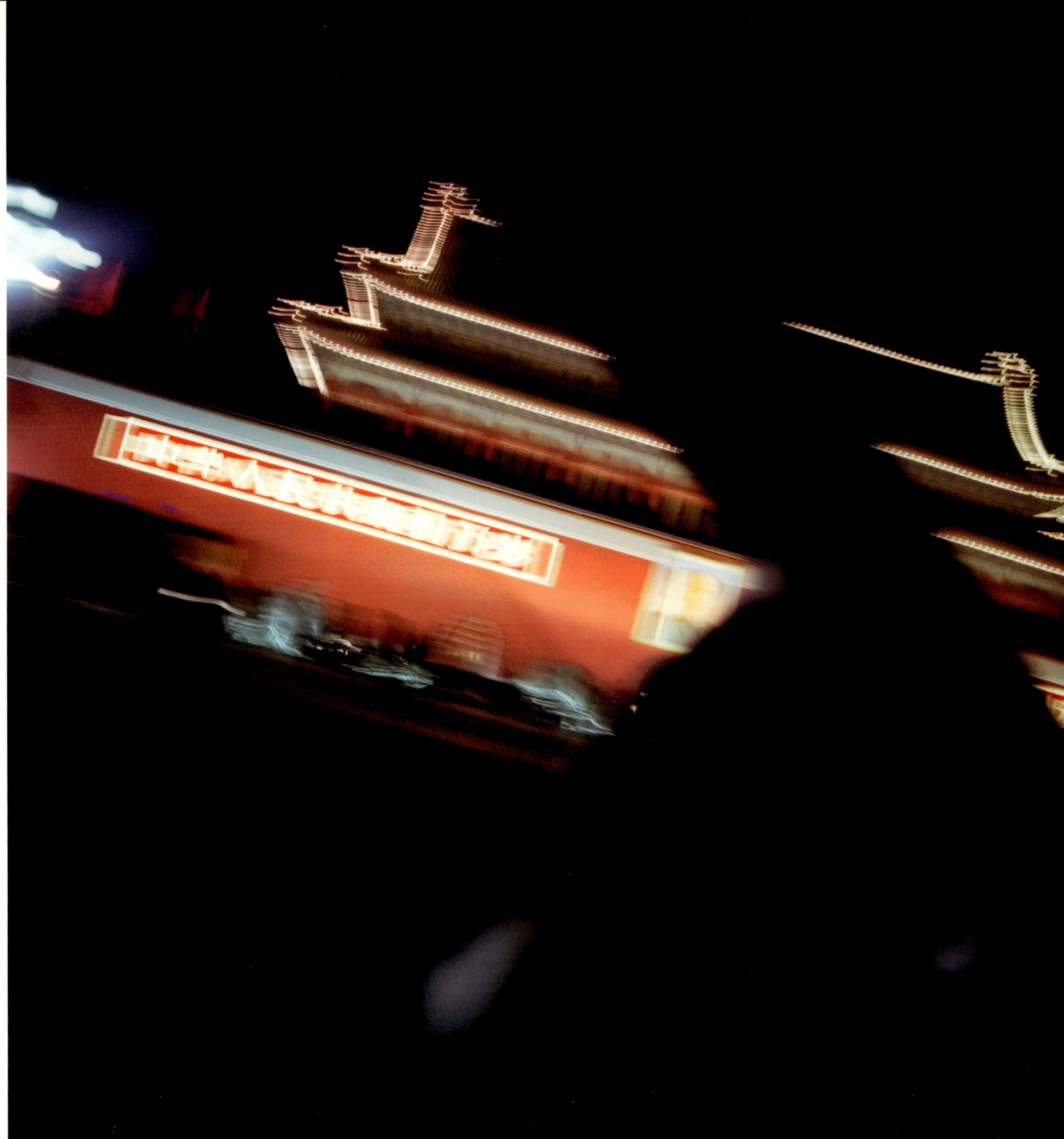

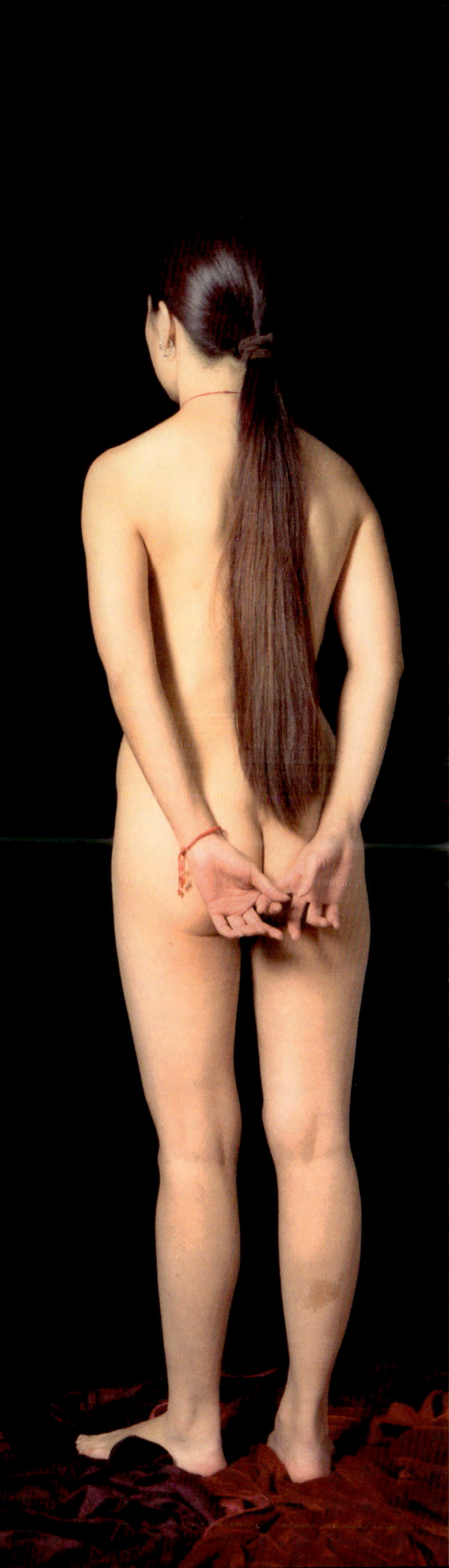

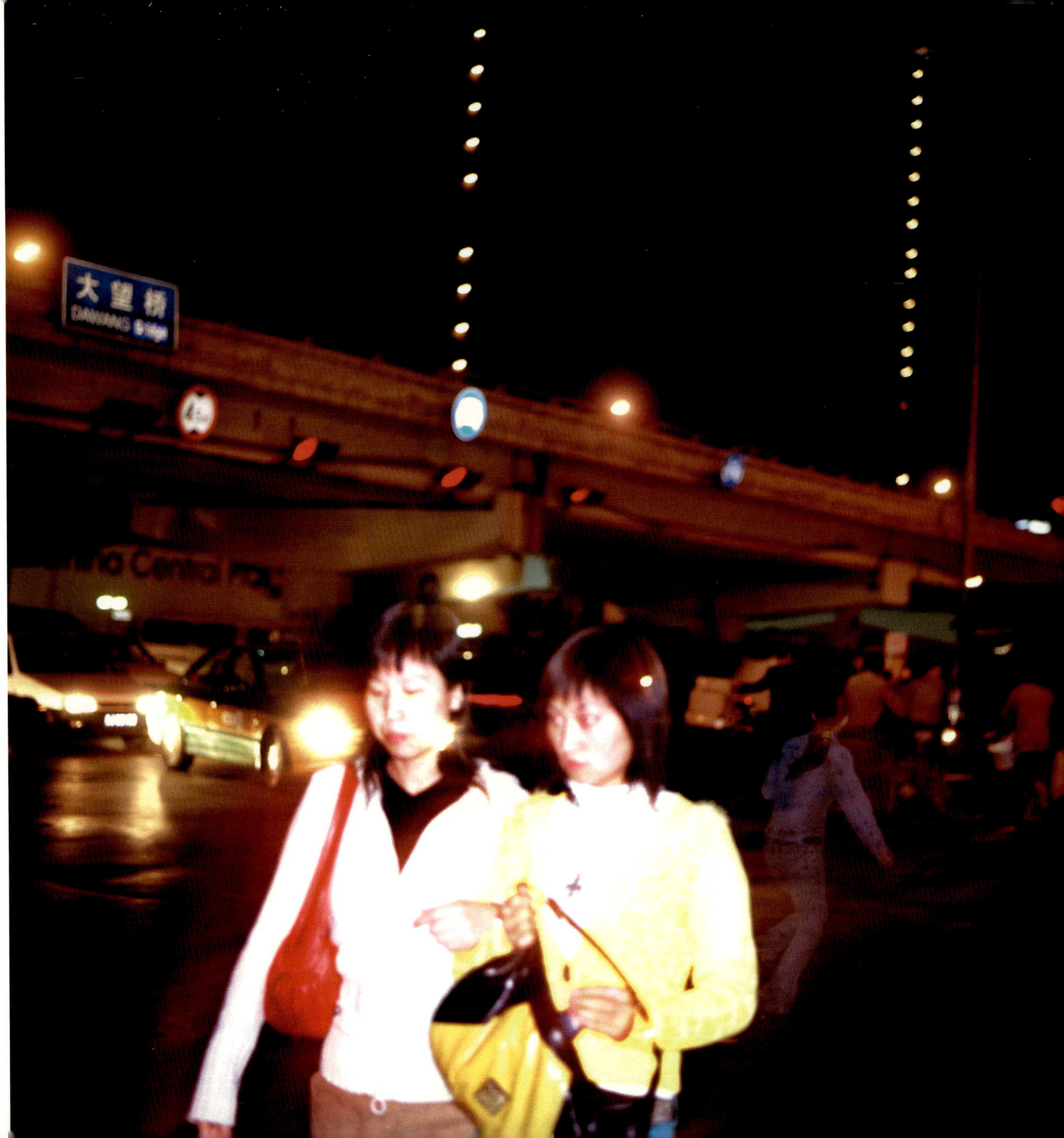
大望桥

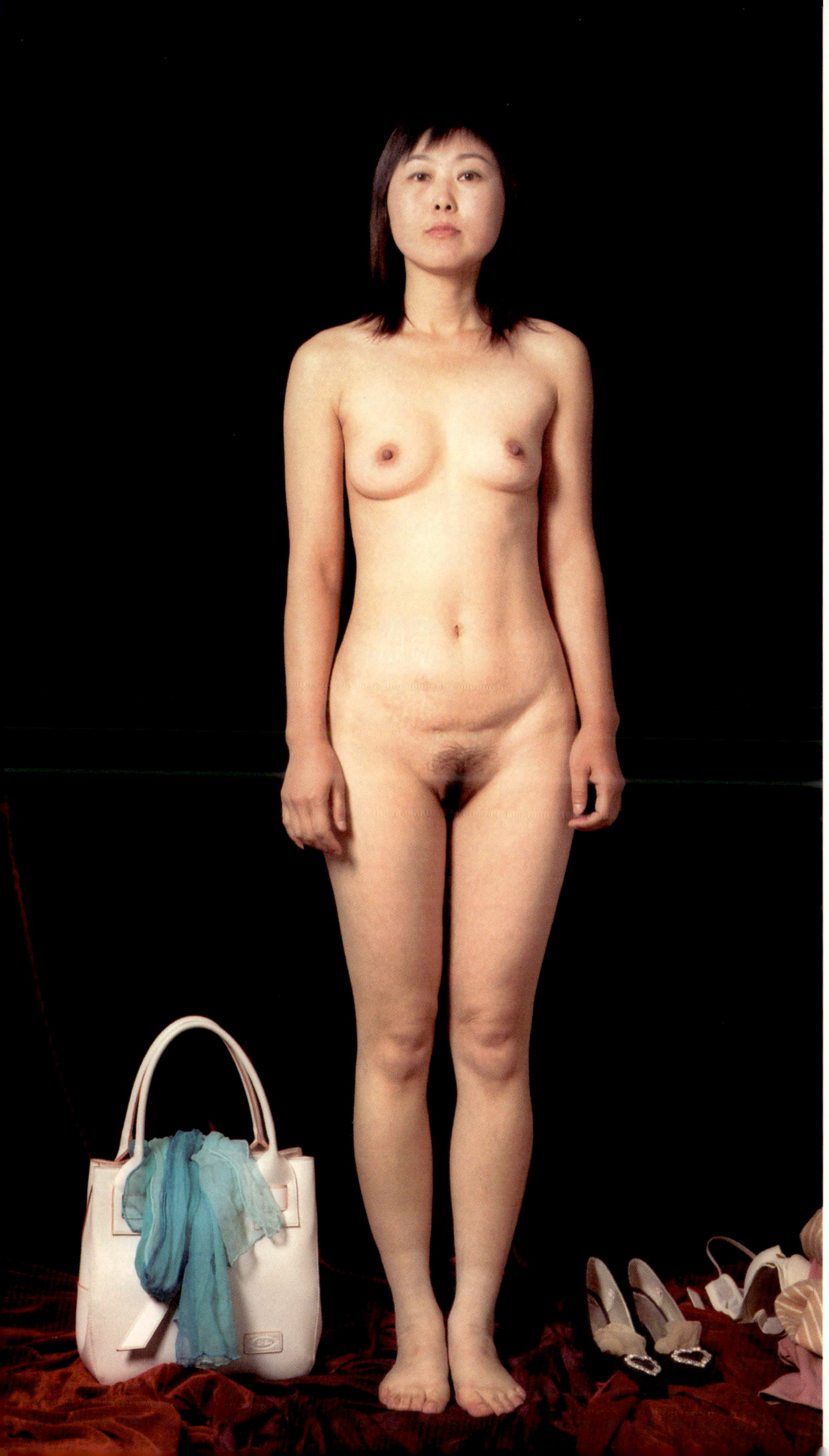

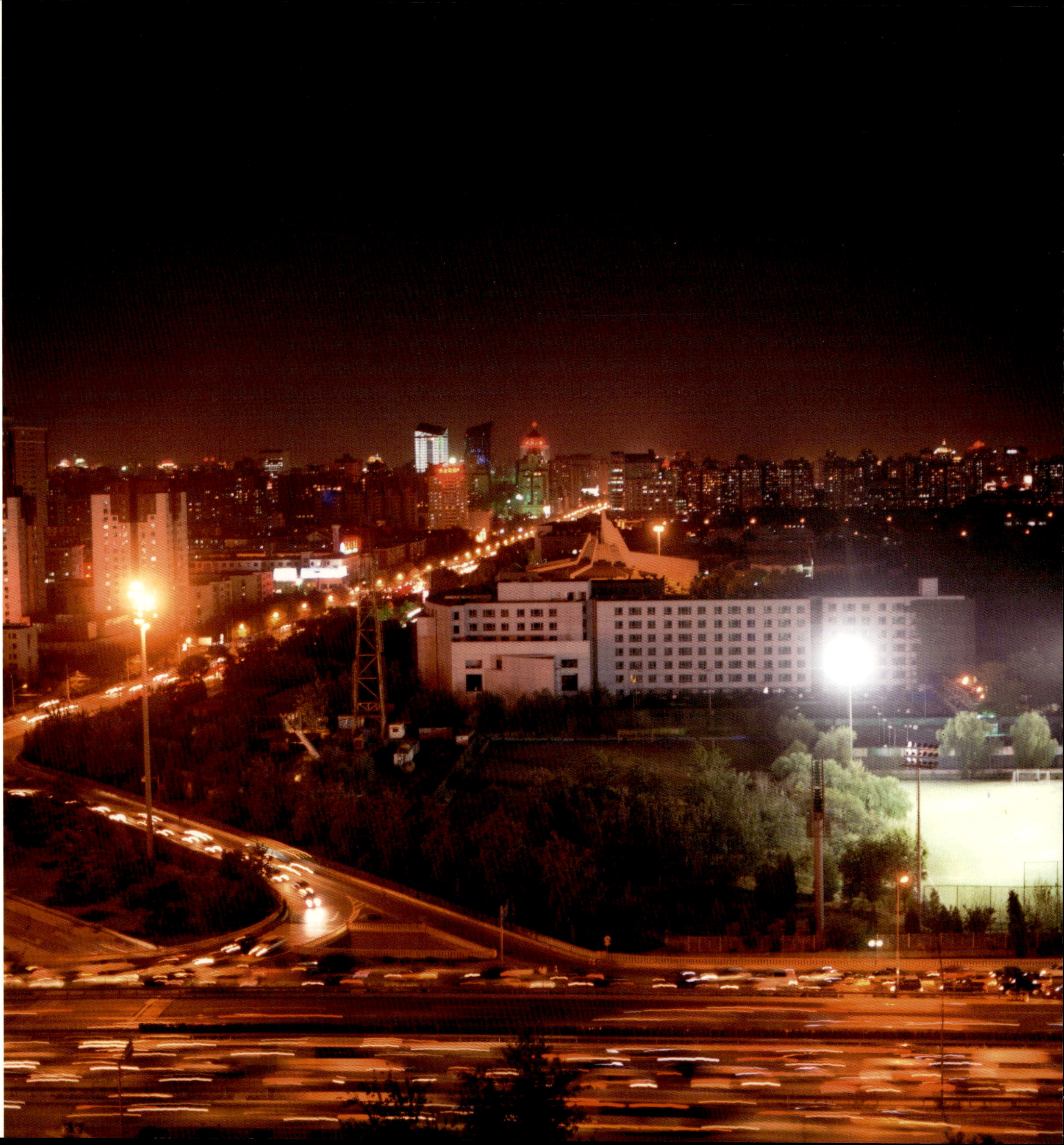

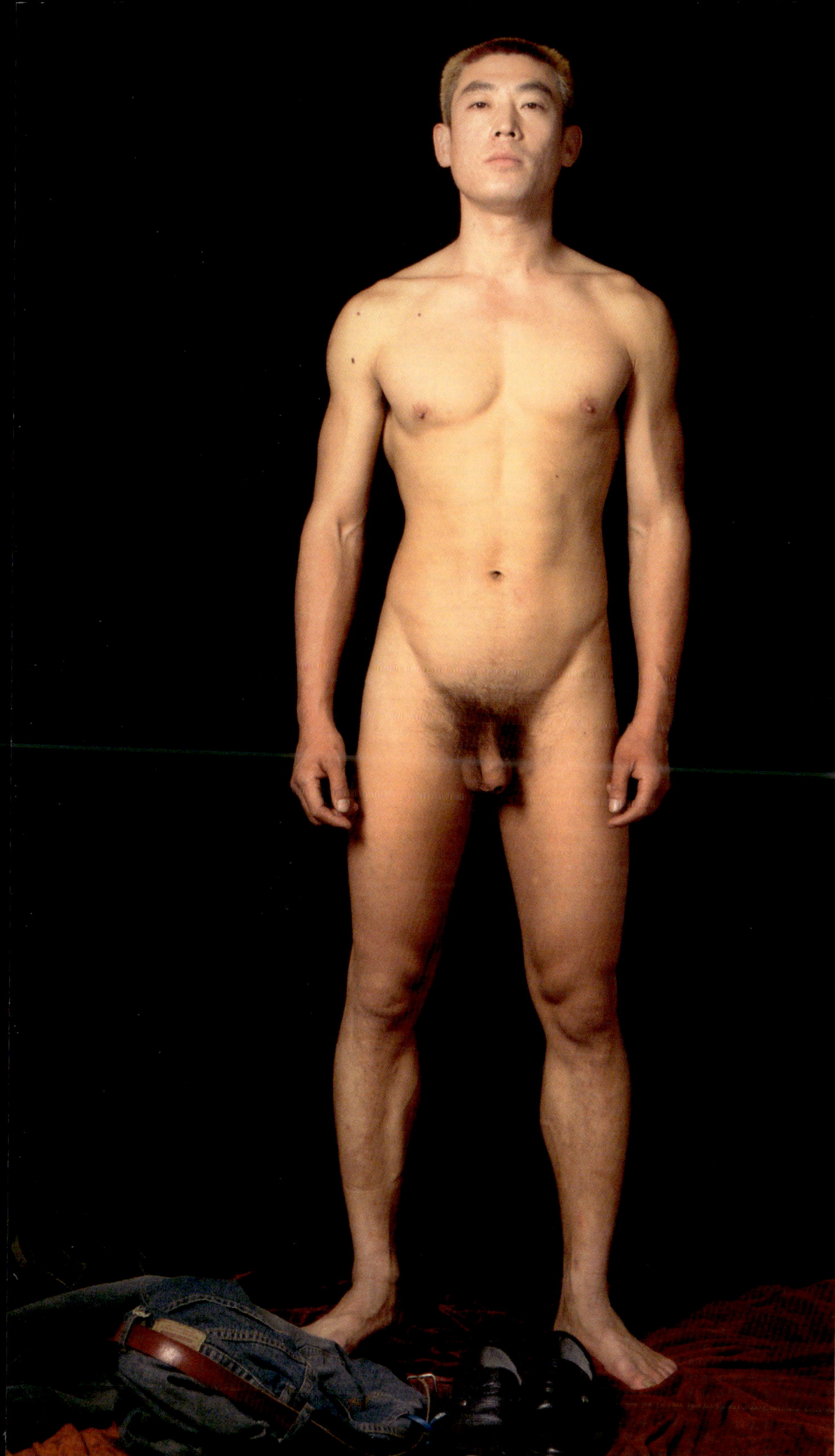

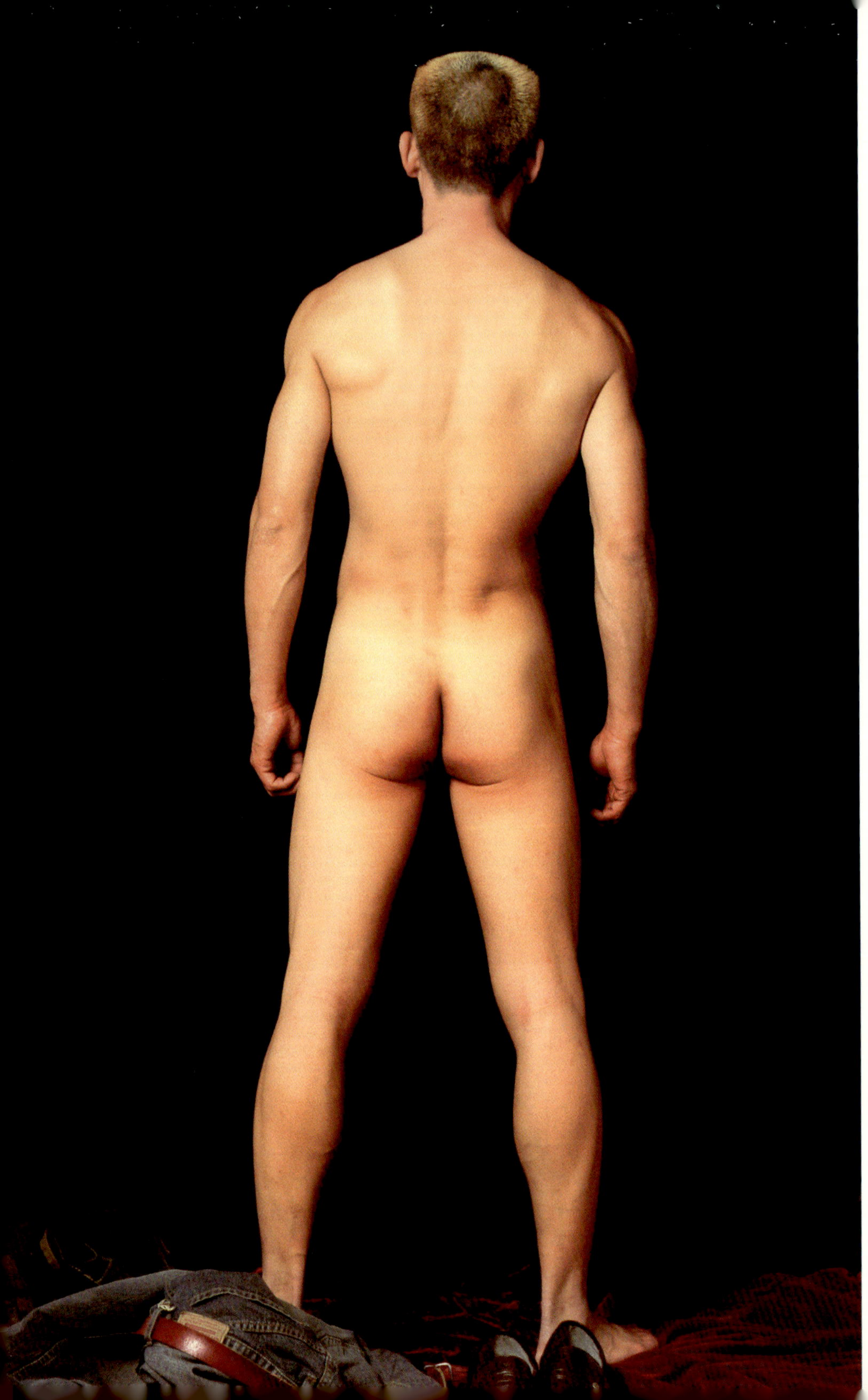

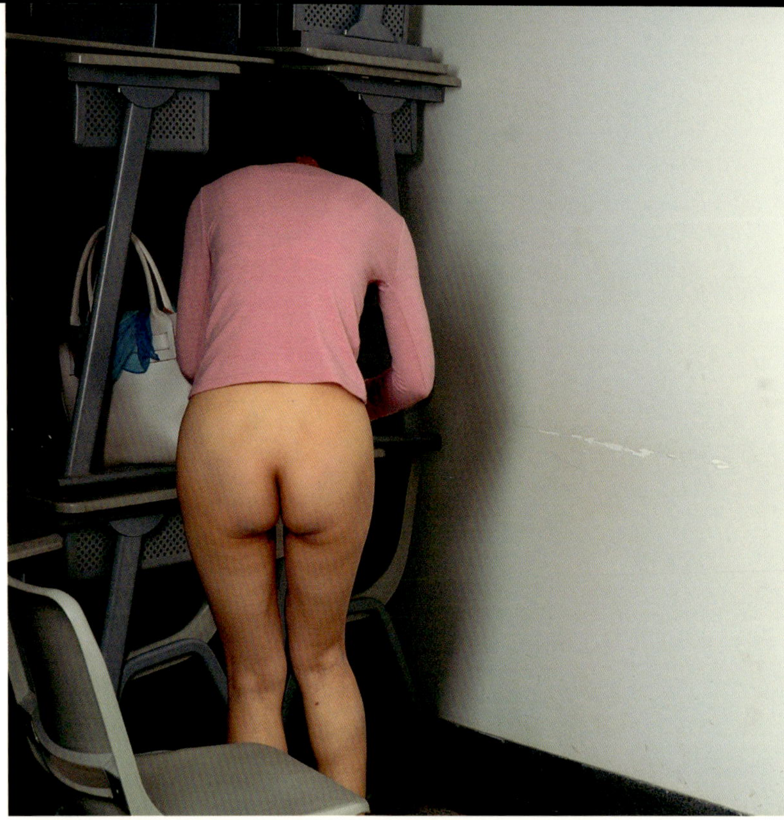

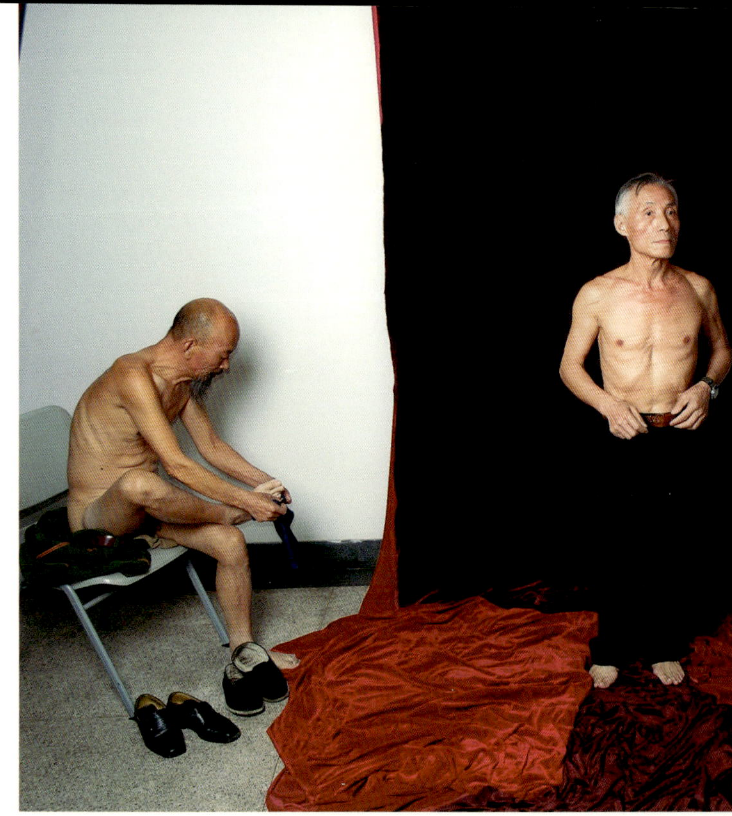

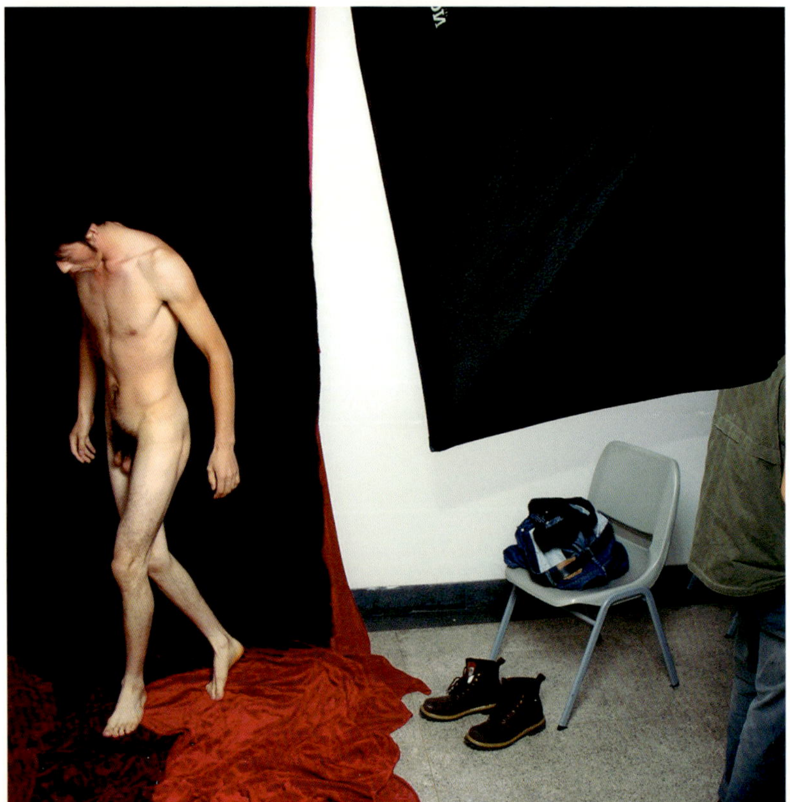

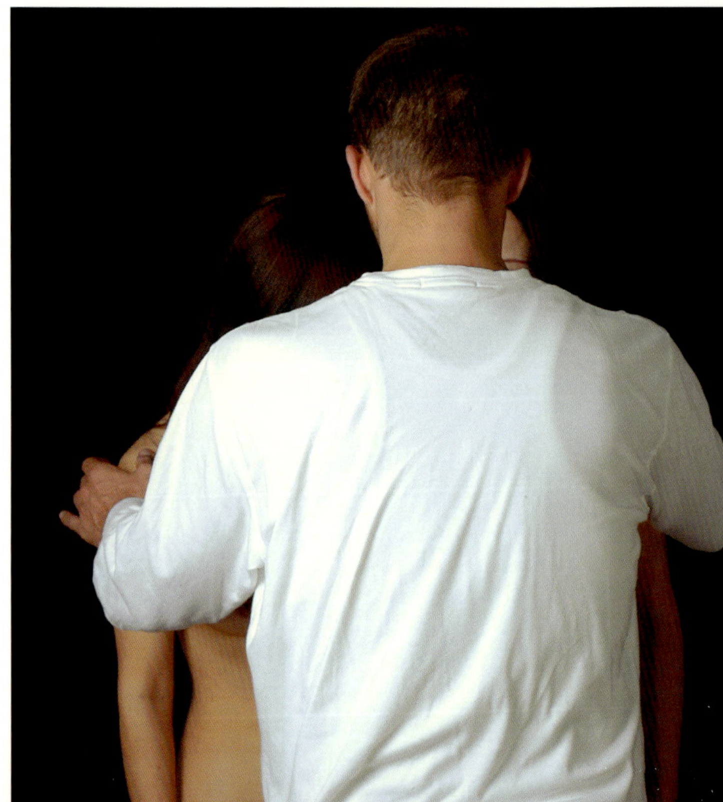

CHINA NAKED

At the age of 19, I had the idea to travel to Africa. I made it to Kenya and Egypt. After a short period I met someone from Brazil, and he invited me to Asia. So I booked a new flight from Cairo to Bangkok. This was in 1991, and Bangkok was an interesting, dirty place full of life. To make it short, after a while in Thailand and Hong Kong I shipped over to China. I took a ferry boat from Hong Kong at night. When I woke up the next morning, I could see the mainland of China on the horizon. I remember it very well. A grey skyline with red flags. It was like watching a black-and-white movie on an old TV.

After I had got a stamp in my passport and entered China, the colors did not change much. At that time, China was a country that reminded me somehow of a washed out uniform. A decade later all of that had vanished. China had become one of the strongest economies in Asia. The grey color had almost vanished and came back only on those days when the wind blew all the dirt of the Chinese industries into the cities. Then even the colors of newly opened restaurants and shops had a problem to fight it.

The Chinese dragon has woken up again. The country that invented the noodles before the Italians even knew how to cook, is one of the places everyone worldwide looks at. But who are they, the Chinese? Do they work more than everyone else worldwide? Do they never sleep? Are they more intelligent than other people on the planet? How do they think? How do they feel and what's their plan for the future? Those questions led me to my project "China Naked". I wanted to photograph them naked, so that everyone could see what they look like and that there is no difference between a Chinese and anyone else throughout the world.

But I did not know that Chinese people don't get naked in front of the camera. I asked my Chinese friends to help me with that project, but on the first evening in Beijing they told me: "Frank, you will never get a Chinese naked in front of your camera." They had also tried it already and succeeded only with bare-breasted women, mostly their own sisters. I did not know about that, and so it took me a while to find 21 Chinese people – all of different age and sex. Right from the beginning, I was only interested in portraying them as nudes. Therefore, I asked them to leave their clothes on the ground, so that everyone could see later how they were clad when they entered the set up studio.

On the other hand, I photographed the cityscapes of Beijing and Shanghai to show the dynamics or the dimension of those places. I traveled quite a lot in my life, but I've never been to a country where you can watch houses grow like mushrooms and see people asking their doctors over a video phone for the right medicine.

So, for sure, the Chinese dragon is consuming everything at the moment and is rapidly getting bigger and bigger. The tragedy now is that Chinese people don't have time to reflect their lifestyle. They just try to catch up with the speed and buy the next fridge or so. It's understandable that if you never had those things before you must have them now. I don't blame them for that. I grew up in the Eastern Bloc and also wanted to have certain things I got later after the Fall of the Wall. But once you have them (by the way, it takes a while), you might find out that this helps only little in life, and then, if you are bright enough, you go back to your own roots.

In the end, I produced the first work on naked Chinese people worldwide. There is no other project like this as far as I know. I also found out that Chinese people need to sleep and don't work much harder or longer than others do. But what makes them so strong is the mass population. There is always someone waiting to carry on if one of the others gets tired.

Frank Rothe

REVEALING ANOTHER ME GENERATION

The makeshift studio, arranged by a Chinese colleague, was in business for just one day. The whole day evolved around intimate short stops of capturing Chinese naked.

They stand as if ready for a doctor's visit or a film casting. No make-up, no arrangement of the draped backdrop, nowhere to place the discarded clothes. There are over 20 people to shoot. One after the other, just like the ongoing new entries of dishes of a good Chinese meal. Hello, nice to meet you, thank you, good bye. They go back to work; the photographer continues to work; and finally the lights go out.

Provocation by using human flesh is always a key to incite curiosity. Even bearing this in mind, Frank Rothe has chosen a genre not yet overdone in China. Friends in China often told him that it was an aim impossible to achieve. All the more reason to pursue it, thought the photographer. [1]

The unclothed are simply staged and very frank. No pun intended here, even though Frank Rothe's portrait themes and style of photography are forthright and seldom evasive. [2] By leaving the clothes on the set, Rothe reveals traces of who we are looking at and emphasizes the expediency of his one-day studio. A Mickey Mouse purse, dusty shoes, a belt, impressions of clothing on skin. The line of a sock, big tennis shoes, a raincoat, black pumps, slippers and a necklace. As with any average group of people we have the confident, the shy, the ambivalent, and the curious.

The "nakedness" in Frank Rothe's works is not just about the portraits. It is about his personal challenge of how to leave a mark as a photojournalist in an overrun setting of "China." The cityscapes are common places or objects which anyone could see if they had a few days or weeks in the capital cities: Tiananmen Square, color coordinated tour groups, newly built train stations, brilliantly lit shopping streets, wide auto routes, Shanghai's Pudong and Bund districts, paper lanterns, a quick step into a Chinese restaurant, a glimpse of old town Shanghai. Rothe made most of the cityscapes as long exposures, pursuing movement as a metaphor for the constant change of the city environment. By choosing images of large open spaces, he expresses the minuteness of human scale compared to his huge subject.

There is something very awesome and distant in the cityscapes. The portraits peer at us. They are the facts. The cityscapes are the studies of the photographer's peering. Temptation, distance, ambiguity. So much to see, so much to record. Trekking through the mega-cities leaves the photographer exposed. It costs him kilos, costs him mornings and nights. Frank Rothe's China is exhilarating and simultaneously unprotected.

When the photographer Felice Beato[3] traveled to China in 1860 as one of the first to photograph the country, he photographed the aftermath of the 2nd Boxer uprising. This was important for the allied western forces to show the devastation and death of the Chinese soldiers back home.
Upon first seeing Frank Rothe's work, I could not help but think of the 180-degree turn of subject matter. 150 years of time and events are part of the places and faces which Rothe photographed. Photography in turn has undergone immense technical but very little stylistic changes. The strength of the portrait of the unknown still fascinates, still informs, still misinforms. The document becomes dearer as time passes. What will Frank Rothe's "China Naked" mean 150 years from now? This alone is more precious to consider than what the photographs bare now.

Celina Lunsford

1 At a festival for Chinese photographers in Beijing at the end of 2006 the artist Rong Rong showed nudes including self-portraits; and another photographer, Xu Yong, also uses the nude symbolically in staged photography. These are just a few examples.

2 Two other portrait series examples from Frank Rothe are "German Guns," where he shot young and old holding their weapons of sport, and "Going Out," where he made photo-essays of different Berliners getting ready to go out into town and then returning home to bed.

3 Felice Beato, one of the most accomplished portrait photographers of all time, known as well for landscapes and architecture, is also considered one of the first photojournalists.

ON THE INTERTWINING OF NAKEDNESS, TRUTH AND REALITY

China is the Economic Miracle nation of the new century. With its 1.3 billion inhabitants, the Red Dragon is beginning to make a lasting mark on the face of the current era. Frank Rothe has developed his as yet unpublished project "China Naked" as a mixture of landscape picture and individual portrait that's bursting with life, raising questions about the hectic pace in China's dynamic mass society as well as about the status of a naked self plagued by doubt and yet fighting for the spotlight.

Observing a foreign world and culture from the outside and capturing it on film to fulfill an assignment, or following one's own inner voice to develop a concept that transforms the other according to one's own perceptions, are two different things. Frank Rothe's monumental image series "China Naked" speaks of a personal, European point of view as well as of the non-European perspective. Just as we as observers determine what is at the center and what remains on the periphery, the non-European standpoint also exercises its effect on us. Beyond the horizon, at the edges of the world, there are both hells and heavens. From the perspective of the numerous cultures that regard themselves as being at the center of the world, the incomprehensibilities at that world's fringes seem to be accumulating. This goes for both the countries of Europe with their various points of view as well as for China.

Alterity studies assume that the other is always a construct, that it is always constituted in its own present time, that it first describes this present itself, and makes it possible to describe it at all, and that the construction of the other is always motivated and thus shaped by personal interests.
"China Naked," like every picture having to do with the theme of identity and alterity, can thus be nothing more than a conglomerate of ideological assumptions, regardless of the insight that photographs and television images with their high rate of speed anyway tend to glue the gaze to the surface, seducing and obfuscating perception. [1]

The series "China Naked" stands at the center of various aesthetic, cultural and historical charge fields in which the sub-themes of "urban transformation" and "nakedness" are inscribed. The images are all diptychs composed of two types of images. Rothe created both staged photos in which he asked his Chinese subject to disrobe for the camera, and also cast his gaze on the Moloch that is the Chinese city, resulting in juxtapositions with a slightly symbolic charge. We see nothing of the rapid pace of city life, of pollution, corruption and speculation; no split personalities are revealed to the camera, but we can sense in the shimmering images the uncloaking of a society.

A not insignificant portion of current Chinese image production deals with manifestations of the country's own culture, featuring hollow motifs blown up to gigantic size as a critique of the West, as a way of re-imagining forms of community. On the streets of the big cities, Western advertising strategies are being imitated in what to our eyes looks like a sentimental effort by the Chinese to violate the taboos of their own community life. One can sense that Western advertising concepts and the Western way of seeing are viewed in China with respect as displaying innovation, high quality and a consistent style, while at the same time they are still suspected of spreading socially and morally questionable attitudes.

European male and female models in today's ads embody for the Chinese unbridled and erotic exoticism, something inflammatory that is sneaking under the skin of the public image of the body. The West is still viewed as the modern model, with Chinese women in particular striving to emulate its ideals of beauty. Added to this is the fact that a shift in eating habits is provoking rapid changes in body size and proportions in China, while fashion trends from the West (including rather dubious ones), the way of looking at the body – with both voyeurism and dramatization – as well as new definitions of health are spreading more quickly to even the remoter regions thanks to the uncomplicated appropriation options made possible by today's media.

The individualistic Western lifestyle and the trend toward singledom, involving of course a focus on the freedoms and rights of the individual, are deemed in Chinese party propaganda as lacking in solidarity, as negative, and are thus visualized as being incompatible counter-images to Chinese society.

The subjects in "China Naked" appear without clothes not because they want to, but upon the request of the photographer. It is a hallmark of European culture to be fixated in various ways on nakedness. In China, nakedness does not play such a pronounced role in art and society, perhaps because there the body is not regarded anatomically but rather according to the aspect of energy. In the Chinese conception, the body is not a dynamic composite of individual limbs, but instead a holistic capacity. European culture in all its various facets developed out of the nude and its proportions – both before and after the Greeks – a neutral idea of beauty, of health and well-being, which was passed down especially through art and is still enshrined in our perceptions today. In the art academies of China and Japan, however, young students critical of the Western influence are today increasingly calling into question the character of East-West relations in connection with their own historic roots.
In China, the nude as bearer of the ideal of beauty in form and being does not exist, but Chinese students nevertheless still learn to draw the nude from plaster casts of classic Greek statues.

In a lecture in Berlin in May 2001, French philosopher François Jullien juxtaposed the "nude" as concept in the Occidental tradition with the "thread" in Chinese philosophy: "European culture is fixated on the nude just as philosophy is on truth. The nude is just as central to the teaching of art as logic is to philosophy." [2]
In China, by contrast, nakedness is regarded as superficial and unattractive. Rather, it is the veiled, hidden, mystical human body that is the source of inspiration and fantasy. The naked subjects in Frank Rothe's images are thus taking on a role that is alien to them; they are trying out something that is other, something opposite to their own view of the body, stepping over the threshold into a different way of thinking. Those who knew the country in the days of Communist rule and revisit post-modern China today will learn something about the realistic attitude of the young Chinese, who accept what are objectively incompatible elements with a shrug and then get on with their lives.

Just how rapidly China's transformation is proceeding naturally cannot be intimated from the legendary nude beach that nudists applied for years ago in the province of Zhejiang, a project that was scrapped shortly before being opened to the public. Similar plans came up against resistance from the authorities in northern Heilongjiang and in Sichuan as well. Although public exposure in Hong Kong is punishable by up to six months' imprisonment or a 97-euro fine, a group of activists there has been trying since 2005 to open their own nudist club. The outcome of their efforts remains to be seen.

That the transformation in China is a profound one is demonstrated more clearly by a comparison between the photos Heinz von Perckhammer (1895 – 1965) took during a trip to South China and Macao in the late 1920s and the images in "China Naked." For the images in his book, titled "Edle Nacktheit in China" ("The Culture of the Nude in China") [3], Perckhammer persuaded Chinese prostitutes in Macao to pose for his camera. The results, with their florid sepia tone, are part of a soft porn production in which the subjects are asked to please hold still. Old Europe indulges itself fully in its intoxication with exotic Asian sinfulness. The images we see here of enigmatic China are suggestive of "untouched nature" and the curviness of the noble savages. Fallen nature worshippers. The Pocahontas syndrome as paradigm. The conditions under which Perckhammer took these photos do not enter into the picture. His images are free of any hint of their problematic nature, making them all the more libidinous in their close scanning of the female body. Perckhammer's photographic gaze, while hypocritically pretending to inwardness, finds here a colonial home where it can disport itself in primitive Chinese climes.

By contrast, the young Chinese men and women who let Rothe photograph them without making a fuss are the protagonists of a rare, self-assured exercise in crossing boundaries, having divested themselves of their outer shell. Rothe does not purport to be investigating anything, and neither does he invent. He composes, builds and lets random occurrences unfold their own effects. For him, what is real is the foundation of the artistic process.
By questioning the Chinese relationship to nudity in the country's rapidly changing metropolises in "China Naked," Frank Rothe encourages us to turn around and consider more closely the foundations of our own European traditions and ways of thinking, our philosophy of being, and our ideal of freedom.
Rothe's images ask to be read, not merely looked at, something like the way Chinese characters do not denote the sounds of the language but rather express themselves in imagery – every single icon a picture.

Christoph Tannert

1 *"Photography concentrates one's eye on the superficial. For that reason it obscures the hidden life, which glimmers through the outlines of things like a play of light and shade," Gustav Janouch, Conversations with Kafka, quoted in: Susan Sontag, On Photography, New York: Farrar, Straus and Giroux, 1977.*

2 *Cf. François Jullien, The Impossible Nude. Chinese Art and Western Aesthetics, Chicago: University of Chicago Press, 2007.
Cf. François Jullien, In Praise of Blandness. Proceeding from Chinese Thought and Aesthetics, New York: Zone Books, 2004.*

3 *Heinz von Perckhammer, The Culture of the Nude in China, Berlin/Zurich: Eigenbrödler Verlag, 1928, with 32 photographs.*

CHINA NAKED

Mit 19 Jahren reiste ich nach Afrika. Ich kam bis nach Kenia und Ägypten. In Nairobi traf ich jemanden aus Brasilien, der mich nach Asien einlud. Also buchte ich einen Flug von Kairo nach Bangkok. Das war 1991 und Bangkok war ein interessanter Ort – dreckig und voller Leben. Um es zu kurz zu machen – ich verbrachte einige Zeit in Thailand und Hongkong und fuhr dann weiter nach China mit der Nachtfähre von Hongkong rüber aufs Festland. Als ich am nächsten Morgen aufwachte, sah ich die chinesische Küste am Horizont. Ich kann mich sehr gut daran erinnern. Eine graue Silhouette durchbrochen von roten Fahnen, ähnlich einem Schwarz-Weiß-Film, der über einen alten Bildschirm flimmert.

Die Farben veränderten sich nicht, nachdem ich meinen Stempel in den Pass gedrückt bekam und nach China eingereist war. China hatte große Ähnlichkeit mit einer alten verwaschenen Uniform. Zehn Jahre später gab es dieses Land nicht mehr. China, heute eines der stärksten Wirtschaftsmächte Asiens, hat sein eigenes Grau erfolgreich verdrängt. Nur hin und wieder, besonders an den Tagen, wenn der Wind den Staub der chinesischen Industrie durch die Städte bläst, kehrt es für Momente zurück. In diesen Augenblicken fällt es auch den Farben der neuen Restaurants und Geschäfte schwer sich durchzusetzen.

Der chinesische Drachen ist erwacht. Die gesamte Welt schaut auf dieses Land, das die Nudel erfand, lange bevor die Italiener überhaupt kochen konnten. Aber wer sind die Chinesen? Arbeiten sie mehr als andere Menschen im Rest der Welt? Schlafen sie nie? Sind sie intelligenter? Wie denken sie, was fühlen sie und welche Pläne haben sie für die Zukunft? Diese Fragen inspirierten mich zu dem Projekt „China Naked". Deshalb wollte ich sie nackt fotografieren, so dass jeder sehen kann, wie sie aussehen und dass es keinen Unterschied gibt zwischen einem Chinesen und irgendjemand sonst auf der Welt. Was ich nicht wusste, Chinesen lassen sich nicht nackt fotografieren.

Ich bat meine chinesischen Kollegen, mir bei dem Projekt zu helfen. Doch schon am ersten Abend in Peking sagten sie zu mir: „Frank, du wirst einen Chinesen niemals nackt vor die Kamera bekommen." Sie hatten es auch schon probiert. Das Ergebnis waren hauptsächlich Bilder von Frauen mit entblößter Brust – meist die eigene Schwester. Es kostete mich einiges an Zeit und Kraft bis ich 21 Chinesen gefunden hatte – Männer und Frauen unterschiedlichen Alters. Von Anfang an war ich nur an Nudeporträts interessiert. Deshalb bat ich sie, ihre Kleider am Boden liegen zu lassen, damit später deutlich sichtbar sein würde, wie sie gekleidet waren, als sie ins Studio kamen.

Die Akte komponierte ich mit Stadtlandschaften von Peking und Shanghai, in denen ich größtenteils mit Langzeitbelichtungen die Dynamik und die Dimensionen der Städte zeigen wollte. Also auf der einen Seite die Größe eines Ortes und auf der anderen Seite das kleinere Individuum, das in den Diptics von meinen angelegten Proportionen dennoch einen großen Platz finden sollte.

Auf meinen bisherigen Reisen war ich in noch keinem Land, in dem man sehen konnte, wie Häuser über Nacht immer größer werden und Menschen ihre Ärzte über Video-Telefone konsultieren. Bei diesem Wachstum ist es eine Tragödie, dass die Chinesen keine Zeit haben über ihre Lebensweise nachzudenken. Sie versuchen derzeit einfach nur mit ihrer eigenen Entwicklung mitzuhalten, um sich den nächsten Kühlschrank zu kaufen. Es ist verständlich, dass man Dinge, die man nie hatte, sofort haben muss. Ich werfe ihnen das nicht vor. Ich bin im Ostblock aufgewachsen und mir ging es ähnlich. Der Wunsch nach Konsum, solange man ihn nicht leben kann, übt großen Sog aus. Wird die Kauflust erst einmal befriedigt (was hin und wieder dauern kann), findet man vielleicht heraus, dass diese Art von Befriedigung nur wenig weiterhilft.

Soweit ich weiß, ist „China Naked" die erste Arbeit weltweit, die so viele nackte Chinesen vereint. Während meiner Aufenthalte habe ich übrigens herausgefunden, dass Chinesen genauso viel Schlaf brauchen und auch nicht viel mehr arbeiten als andere Menschen. Was sie aber so stark macht ist die Bevölkerungszahl. Es ist immer jemand da, der weitermachen kann, wenn ein anderer müde wird.

Frank Rothe

EINE ANDERE ICH-GENERATION ENTDECKEN

Das provisorische Studio, das ein chinesischer Kollege eingerichtet hatte, existierte nur einen Tag lang. An diesem Tag drehte sich alles darum, nackte Chinesen in intimen Momentaufnahmen festzuhalten.

Sie stehen da, als hätten sie sich auf einen Arztbesuch oder ein Film-Casting vorbereitet. Kein Make-up, keine Gestaltung des Hintergrunds, kein Platz für die abgelegte Kleidung. Über zwanzig Menschen sind zu fotografieren. Einer nach dem anderen, genau wie die ständig neu aufgetragenen Gerichte eines guten chinesischen Essens. Guten Tag, sehr angenehm, danke schön, auf Wiedersehen. Sie gehen zurück zur Arbeit, der Fotograf arbeitet weiter und schließlich gehen die Scheinwerfer aus.

Die Provokation durch nackte Haut ist immer ein Mittel, die Neugier anzuregen. Aber selbst wenn man das bedenkt, hat Frank Rothe ein Genre gewählt, das in China noch nicht überstrapaziert ist. Freunde in China haben ihm häufig gesagt, diese Idee sei unmöglich umzusetzen. Umso mehr Grund es zu versuchen, dachte der Fotograf. [1]

Die Unbekleideten sind schlicht inszeniert und sehr offen. Das ist kein Wortspiel, denn Themen und Stil von Frank Rothes Porträts sind sehr freimütig und nur selten vage. [2] Indem er die Kleidung mit abbildet, zeigt Rothe Aspekte der Personen, die wir anschauen, und betont die Zweckmäßigkeit seines Ein-Tages-Studios. Eine Mickey-Mouse-Handtasche, staubige Schuhe, ein Gürtel, Abdrücke von Kleidung auf der Haut. Der Rand einer Socke, große Turnschuhe, ein Regenmantel, schwarze Pumps, Hausschuhe und eine Halskette. Wie in jeder beliebigen Gruppe von Menschen erkennen wir die Selbstbewussten, die Schüchternen, die Unentschiedenen und die Neugierigen.

Um Nacktheit geht es nicht nur in Frank Rothes Porträts, sondern auch in seinem persönlichen Anspruch, dem überlaufenen Motiv „China" seinen Stempel als Fotojournalist aufzudrücken. Die Stadtansichten zeigen bekannte Orte oder Objekte, die jeder sehen könnte, der sich für ein paar Tage oder Wochen in den großen Städten aufhält: den Tiananmen Platz, nach Farben geordnete Touristengruppen, neu erbaute Bahnhöfe, hell erleuchtete Einkaufsstraßen, breite Autobahnen, den Pudong und Bund Distrikt in Shanghai, Papierlaternen, einen kurzen Abstecher in ein chinesisches Restaurant, einen Blick auf die Altstadt von Shanghai. Rothe hat die meisten Stadtansichten mit langen Belichtungszeiten aufgenommen, zeigt Bewegung als Metapher für die ständigen Veränderungen des städtischen Umfelds. Indem er Bilder von großen, offenen Räumen aufnimmt, zeigt er die Winzigkeit des Menschen im Verhältnis zu seinem riesigen Motiv.

Die Stadtansichten strahlen etwas Ehrfurcht gebietendes und Distanziertes aus. Die Porträts schauen uns an. Sie sind Tatsachen. Die Stadtansichten dokumentieren den Blick des Fotografen. Versuchung, Distanz, Vieldeutigkeit. So viel zu sehen, so viel aufzunehmen. Das Wandern durch die Megacitys entblößt den Fotografen. Es kostet ihn Kilos, kostet ihn Tage und Nächte. Frank Rothes China ist berauschend und gleichzeitig ungeschützt.

Als der Fotograf Felice Beato [3] 1860 als einer der ersten seiner Zunft durch China reiste, fotografierte er die Auswirkungen des zweiten Boxeraufstands. Den westlichen Kolonialmächten war es wichtig, die Verheerungen und den Tod der chinesischen Soldaten zu Hause zu zeigen.
Als ich Frank Rothes Bilder zum ersten Mal sah, drängte sich mir unweigerlich der Gedanke auf, dass sich die Perspektive auf das Motiv um 180 Grad gedreht hat. 150 Jahre Geschichte sind Teil der Orte und Gesichter, die Rothe fotografiert hat.
Die Fotografie selbst hat in dieser Zeit immense technische Veränderungen durchgemacht, während ihr Stil sich kaum gewandelt hat. Das Porträt des Unbekannten besitzt noch immer die Kraft zu fesseln, zu informieren, zu täuschen. Was wird Frank Rothes „China Naked“ in 150 Jahren bedeuten? Allein die Vorstellung davon ist wertvoller als das, was die Fotografien jetzt offenbaren.

Celina Lunsford

1 Ende 2006 zeigte der Künstler Rong Rong bei einem Festival für chinesische Fotografie in Peking Aktfotos, u.a. auch Selbstporträts. Auch der Fotograf Xu Yong setzt den Akt symbolisch in inszenierten Bildern ein. Dies sind nur ein paar Beispiele.

2 Zwei weitere beispielhafte Porträtserien von Frank Rothe sind „German Guns“, Fotografien junger und alter Menschen mit ihren Sportwaffen, und „Going Out“, eine Reihe von Fotoessays, die zeigen, wie sich Berliner zum Ausgehen vorbereiten und dann nach Hause ins Bett zurückkehren.

3 Felice Beato, einer der fähigsten Porträtfotografen aller Zeiten, auch bekannt für seine Landschafts- und Architekturaufnahmen, gilt als einer der ersten Fotojournalisten.

ÜBER DAS INEINANDER VON NACKTHEIT, WAHRHEIT UND WIRKLICHKEIT

China ist das Wirtschaftswunderland des neuen Jahrhunderts. Mit seinen 1,3 Milliarden Einwohnern beginnt der rote Drache das Gesicht der neuen Zeit nachhaltig zu prägen. Sein bisher nicht veröffentlichtes Projekt „China Naked" hat Frank Rothe in einer lebensprallen Mischung aus Landschaftsbild und Individualporträt entwickelt, die Fragen nach der Lebensgeschwindigkeit in der dynamischen chinesischen Massengesellschaft stellt und auch nach dem Status des von Zweifeln wie Selbstdarstellungsinteressen entblößten Ich.

Die Welt, das Fremde von außen zu beobachten und auftragsgemäß abzulichten oder der eigenen, inneren Stimme folgend ein Konzept zu entwickeln, in dem man sich das Andere anverwandelt, sind zweierlei Dinge. Frank Rothes monumentale Bildserie „China Naked" spricht vom eigenen, europäischen Blick ebenso wie von der außereuropäischen Wahrnehmung. So wie wir Zentrum und Peripherie bestimmen, setzt sich auch die außereuropäische Wahrnehmung in Bezug auf uns durch. Hinter dem Horizont, an den Rändern der Welt sind Höllen und Paradiese gleichermaßen verortet. Aus der Perspektive der zahlreichen Weltmittelpunkt-Kulturen häufen sich am Rande der Welt die Unverständlichkeiten. Das gilt für die Länder Europas mit ihren unterschiedlichen Perspektiven ebenso wie für China.
Die Alteritätsforschung geht davon aus, dass das Andere grundsätzlich immer konstruiert ist, dass es sich immer an der eigenen Gegenwart konstituiert, dass es diese selbst zuallererst beschreibt und überhaupt zu beschreiben ermöglicht, und dass die Konstruktion des Anderen immer von einem eigenen Interesse motiviert und auch entsprechend gestaltet ist.
„China Naked" kann also, so wie jedes Bild im Themenkreis von Eigenheit und Fremdheit, nur ein Konglomerat ideologischer Annahmen sein, unabhängig von der Einsicht, dass Fotografien und Fernsehbilder sowieso den Blick mit Hochgeschwindigkeit an der Oberfläche fesseln, verführen und vernebeln. [1]
Die Serie „China Naked" steht im Zentrum unterschiedlicher ästhetischer, kultureller und historischer Spannungsfelder, in die die Subthemen „Städtischer Wandel" und „Nacktheit" eingeschrieben sind. Alle Bilder folgen einer konsequenten Zweiteilung. Frank Rothe hat einerseits Fotos durch Inszenierung erarbeitet, indem er Chinesen und Chinesinnen bat, vor der Kamera ihre Kleider abzulegen, andererseits hat er seinen Blick auf den Moloch Stadt in seiner chinesischen Variante gerichtet und Bilder mit leicht symbolischer Aufladung entstehen lassen. Wir sehen nichts von Rasanz, Umweltverschmutzung, Bestechung und Spekulation, keine Persönlichkeitsspaltungen vor der Kamera, aber wir fühlen im Flirren der Aufnahmen die Entschleierung der Gesellschaft.

Ein nicht unwesentlicher Teil der gegenwärtigen chinesischen Bildproduktion verhandelt Erscheinungen der eigenen Kultur in hohlen, gigantisch aufgeblasenen Motiven als Kritik am Westen, um Formen von Gemeinschaft zu re-imaginieren. Im Straßenbild der großen Städte wird andererseits augenfällig, dass Werbestrategien des Westens abgekupfert werden, um damit auf für unsere Augen sentimentale Art Tabus des eigenen Gemeinwesens zu brechen. Daran lässt sich ablesen, wie westliche Werbekonzepte und westliches Sehen in China achtungsvoll als innovativ, qualitätvoll und stilkonsequent gelten, gleichzeitig in der chinesischen Wahrnehmung in ihnen aber auch sozial und moralisch bedenkliche Einstellungsdispositionen registriert werden. Männliche und weibliche europäische Models verkörpern in der aktuellen Werbung das Ungezügelte und erotisch Exotische, etwas Aufrührerisches, das sich subkutan über das Körperbild in die Öffentlichkeit einschleicht. Der Westen gilt nach wie vor als modern, seinen Schönheitsidealen eifern insbesondere chinesische Frauen nach. Hinzu kommt, dass sich durch veränderte Essgewohnheiten die menschlichen Körpermaße und -proportionen in China rapide verändern, Modetrends des Westens (durchaus auch die zweifelhaften), die Art des Blicks auf den Körper, Schaulust und Inszenierung sowie Gesundheitsdefinitionen aufgrund unkomplizierter Aneignungsmöglichkeiten schneller und auch in abgelegenen Regionen eine Chance auf Verbreitung finden. Besonders das Individualistische westlichen Lebensstils und der Trend zur Singlisierung, selbstverständlich auch die Freiheiten und Rechte des Einzelnen, gelten in der chinesischen Parteipropaganda als unsolidarisch und negativ und werden entsprechend visualisiert als inkompatible Gegenbilder zur chinesischen Gesellschaft.

Das Bildpersonal in „China Naked" tritt unbekleidet ins Bild, nicht auf eigenen Wunsch, sondern auf Wunsch des Fotografen. Es ist ein Merkmal der europäischen Kultur, vielseitig auf das Nackte fixiert zu sein. In China findet das Nackte in Kunst und Gesellschaft keine Möglichkeiten, was daran liegen mag, dass der Körper dort nicht anatomisch, sondern energetisch betrachtet wird. Der Körper ist in der chinesischen Vorstellung kein dynamischer Verbund von Einzelgliedmaßen, vielmehr eine ganzheitliche Kapazität. Die europäische Kultur in all ihren Besonderheiten entwickelte vor und nach den Griechen aus dem Nackten und seinen Proportionen eine neutrale Idee des Schönen, des Heilen und Gesunden, die insbesondere über die Kunst bis in die Weihehallen unserer Zeit weitergereicht wurde. Über diesen Weg allerdings auch wieder zurück in die Kunstakademien in China und Japan, wo junge, dem Westen kritisch gegenübertretende Studenten nunmehr vermehrt nach dem Charakter der Ost-West-Beziehungen im Zusammenhang mit den eigenen historischen Wurzeln fragen. In China gibt es das Nackte als Träger des Schönheitsideals der Form und des Seins nicht, trotzdem zeichnen chinesische Studenten nach Gipsabgüssen der griechischen Klassik.

Der französische Philosoph François Jullien stellte bei einem Berliner Vortrag im Mai 2001 das „Nackte" als Begriff der abendländischen Tradition dem „Faden" in der chinesischen Philosophie gegenüber: „Die europäische Kultur ist auf das Nackte fixiert wie die Philosophie auf die Wahrheit. In der Lehre der Kunst ist der Akt so zentral wie die Logik in der Philosophie". [2]
Nacktheit gilt dagegen in China als vordergründig und unattraktiv. Das Verhüllte, Verborgene, Mystische des angezogenen Körpers ist die Quelle der Inspiration und der Fantasie. Die Nackten in Frank Rothes Bildern schlüpfen also in eine Rolle, die nicht ihre eigene ist, sie probieren das Andere aus, auch das körperlich Entgegengesetzte, das Hinüberschreiten in eine andere Denkweise. Wer das von der KP beherrschte und doch postmoderne China heute bereist, erfährt etwas von der realistischen Denkungsart der jungen Chinesen, die objektive Unvereinbarkeiten als solche mit einem lässigen Schulterzucken quittieren und sich dann wieder ihren Tagesgeschäften zuwenden.

Wie rasant sich Chinas Umbruch vollzieht, zeigt sich natürlich nicht an jenem legendären FKK-Strand, den Freikörperaktivisten vor Jahren in der Provinz Zhejiang beantragten und der dann kurz vor der Eröffnung doch wieder geschlossen wurde. Auch im nördlichen Heilongjiang und in Sichuan scheiterten die Pläne am Widerstand der Behörden. Obwohl nacktes Auftreten in der Öffentlichkeit in Hongkong mit bis zu sechs Monaten Haft oder 97 Euro Geldbuße geahndet wird, hofft eine Gruppe von Aktivisten seit 2005 auf die Eröffnung eines eigenen Nudisten-Clubs. Der Ausgang des Verfahrens ist offen.
Wie gravierend die Veränderungen tatsächlich sind, zeigt deutlicher ein Vergleich zwischen den Fotos von Heinz von Perckhammer (1895–1965), die dieser auf einer Reise nach Südchina und Macao in den späten 20er Jahren des vergangenen Jahrhunderts anfertigte, mit den Bildern von „China Naked". Für seine Bilder unter dem Buchtitel „Edle Nacktheit in China" [3] holte Perckhammer chinesische Prostituierte aus Macao vor die Kamera. Die Bilder in schwülstigem Sepia-Ton sind Teil eines Softpornos, in der das Bildpersonal stillhalten muss. Das alte Europa rauscht mächtig ein ins asiatische Sündenbabel. Die Bilder, die wir zu sehen bekommen vom geheimnisvollen China, suggerieren „unberührte Natur" und den Kurvenreichtum der edlen Wilden. Gefallene Naturanbeterinnen. Pocahontas-Syndrom pur. Die Umstände, unter denen Perckhammer fotografiert hat, treten nicht ins Bild. Seine Bilder sind frei von jeglicher Problematisierung, aber dazu umso triebverfangener in der Abtastung des weiblichen Körpers. Der fotografische Blick Perckhammers findet, Innerlichkeit heuchelnd, hier sein koloniales Heim, um sich an chinesischen Urlandschaften zu ergötzen.

Im Gegensatz dazu sind die jungen Chinesen und Chinesinnen, die sich von Frank Rothe unkompliziert ins Bild holen ließen, die Protagonisten eines seltenen, selbstbewussten Grenzgängertums, ihrer äußeren Hülle entledigt. Frank Rothe gibt nicht vor, zu erforschen und er erfindet nichts. Er komponiert, baut und lässt Zufälle ihrer Wirkung wegen stehen. Für ihn ist das Reale das Fundament des künstlerischen Prozesses.
Indem Frank Rothe in „China Naked" das chinesische Verhältnis zum Nackten in den sich rasant verändernden heutigen chinesischen Großstädten befragt, sind wir als Betrachter angehalten, umgekehrt auch Traditionen und Fundamente europäischen Denkens, der Philosophie, des Seins, des Ideals der Freiheit zu befragen.
Frank Rothes Bilder wollen dabei gelesen werden, nicht nur betrachtet, etwa so wie die chinesischen Schriftzeichen nicht die Laute der Sprache nachzeichnen, sondern bildhaften Ausdruck entfalten – jedes einzelne Ikon ein Bild.

Christoph Tannert

1 „Die Fotografie fesselt den Blick an die Oberfläche. Damit vernebelt sie gewöhnlich das verborgene Wesen, das nur wie ein Licht- und Schattenhauch durch die Zügeder Dinge hindurchschimmert.", Gustav Janouch, Gespräche mit Kafka, nach: Susan Sontag, Über Fotografie, Frankfurt/M. 2003, Fischer-Taschenbuch 3022, Erstausgabe 1977.

2 Vgl. François Jullien: Vom Wesen des Nackten, Sequenzia Verlag, München 2003.
Vgl. François Jullien: Über das Fade. Eine Eloge. Zu Denken und Ästhetik in China, Berlin, Merve Verlag 1999.

3 Heinz von Perckhammer, Edle Nacktheit in China, Berlin/Zürich 1928, mit 35 Abbildungen.

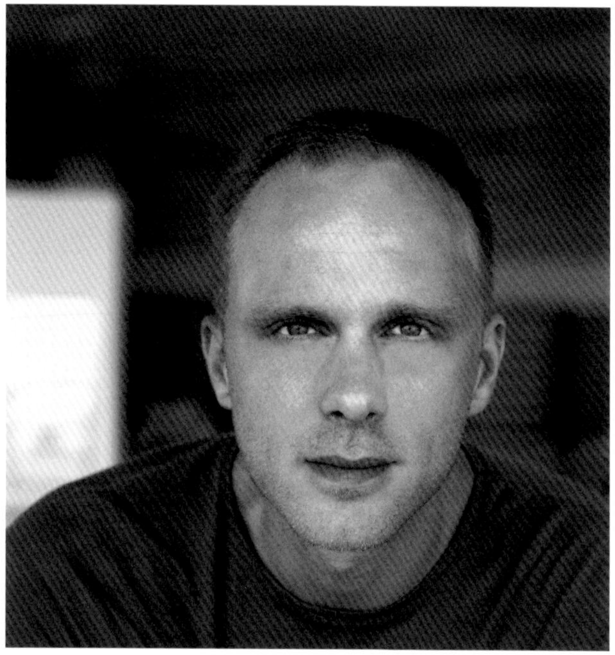

Travel and the desire to experience new cultures are the foundation of Frank Rothe's lifestyle. The extensive traveling he did as a child and youngster led him to become a magazine and newspaper writer at the age of 19. His desire to expand his creative work resulted in him photographing the experiences he was chronicling via writing and using the images to supplement his articles. This decision launched Rothe's career as a photographer. Over the last decade he has been shooting and exhibiting internationally. He has worked on campaigns and as a staff photographer for international and national publications. His work has been awarded and exhibited throughout the world including the USA, Germany, Brazil, South Africa, the Czech Republic, Syria and many other countries.

Der Wunsch in andere Kulturen einzutauchen macht Frank Rothes Lebensstil aus. Ausgedehnte Reisen, die er als Kind und Jugendlicher unternahm, inspirierten ihn im Alter von 19 Jahren dazu, für Zeitungen und Zeitschriften zu schreiben. Weil er sein kreatives Schaffen erweitern wollte, begann er die Erfahrungen, die er schriftlich dokumentierte, auch zu fotografieren. Diese Entscheidung war der Auslöser für seine Karriere als Fotograf. Rothe arbeitet mittlerweile in der ganzen Welt. Seine Arbeiten sind international ausgezeichnet und ausgestellt worden, u.a. in den USA, Deutschland, Brasilien, Polen, Südafrika, Tschechien und Syrien.

I want to thank Klaus Kehrer, Alexa Becker, Jürgen Stephan and all the others from the Kehrer publishing house who did a great job.

I want to thank Celina Lunsford and Christoph Tannert for their great essays.

I want to thank photographer Liu Yiwei for his help in Beijing and my good friend Arianna Rinaldo who put me in contact with him.

I want to thank all my friends from the photography world who took care of me over the last decade and inspired me with their ideas and work.

I want to thank my gallery Camera Work for their support and good advice.

And thank God that I met Jana on this day in East Berlin 17 years ago. I'm happy.

Text / Text: Celina Lunsford, Christoph Tannert
Proofreading / Verlagslektorat: Evelin Selau
Translation / Übersetzung: Franziska Lüdtke, Jennifer Taylor-Gaida
Production / Gesamtherstellung: Kehrer Design Heidelberg
Image processing / Bildbearbeitung: Kehrer Design Heidelberg (Jürgen Stephan, Jürgen Hofmann)
Design / Gestaltung: Kehrer Design Heidelberg (Jürgen Stephan)

Cover picture / Titelbild: Frank Rothe, Lost Image

Bibliographic information published by the Deutsche Nationalbibliothek
The Deutsche Nationalbibliothek lists this publication in the Deutsche Nationalbibliografie;
detailed bibliographic data are available in the Internet at http://dnb.d-nb.de.

Bibliografische Information der Deutschen Nationalbibliothek
Die Deutsche Nationalbibliothek verzeichnet diese Publikation in der Deutschen Nationalbibliografie;
detaillierte bibliografische Daten sind im Internet über http://dnb.d-nb.de abrufbar.

Printed in Germany
www.kehrerverlag.com
www.artbooksheidelberg.com

Kehrer Verlag Heidelberg
ISBN 978-3-939583-11-0